PRAISE FOR *NEW YORK TIMES* BESTSELLING *BATTLE READY*

" . . . Zinni's [descriptions are] vivid . . . [and] down-to-earth. . . . Zinni's views [on the 2003 invasion of Iraq] are persuasive. . . . With luck, we have not seen the last of General Zinni."

—*New York Review of Books*

"The United States could use a few more leaders like Tony Zinni."

—*Times Literary Supplement*

" . . . it is Zinni's 24-page closing statement, 'The Calling,' that will sell the book to nonbuff civilians, summing up his service and the ways in which he feels his generation's legacy is in jeopardy."

—*Publishers Weekly*

"On the Iraq war, [Zinni] insists, 'False rationales presented as justification, a flawed strategy, lack of planning, the unnecessary distraction from real threats, and the unbearable strain dumped on our overstretched military, all of these caused me to speak out.' He warns that military conflict has changed in the twenty-first century and we have been reluctant to recognize it or to acknowledge it. Whether or not readers agree with Zinni, this is a book that demands our attention."

—*Booklist*

THE
BATTLE
FOR
PEACE

THE BATTLE FOR PEACE

A FRONTLINE VISION OF AMERICA'S POWER AND PURPOSE

GENERAL TONY ZINNI

TONY KOLTZ

palgrave
macmillan

BATTLE FOR PEACE
Copyright © Tony Zinni and Tony Koltz, 2006.

First published 2006 by
PALGRAVE MACMILLAN™
175 Fifth Avenue, New York, N.Y. 10010 and
Houndmills, Basingstoke, Hampshire, England RG21 6XS.
Companies and representatives throughout the world.

PALGRAVE MACMILLAN IS THE GLOBAL ACADEMIC IMPRINT OF THE
PALGRAVE MACMILLAN
division of St. Martin's Press, LLC and of Palgrave Macmillan Ltd. Macmillan® is
a registered trademark in the United States, United Kingdom and other countries.
Palgrave is a registered trademark in the European Union and other countries.

ISBN 1-4039-7174-9

Library of Congress Cataloging-in-Publication Data
Zinni, Anthony C.
   The battle for peace : a frontline vision of America's power and purpose /
by Tony Zinni and Tony Koltz.
      p.   cm.
   Includes index.
   ISBN 1-4039-7174-9
   1. United States—Foreign relations—2001—Philosophy.   2. United States—
Foreign relations—1989–   3. United States—Military policy.
4. Post-communism.   5. Peace.   I. Koltz, Tony.   II. Title.

E895.Z56   2006
372.73009'0511—dc22

                                                                                      2005056607

A catalogue record for this book is available from the British Library.

Design by Letra Libre.

First edition: April 2006
10 9 8 7 6 5 4 3 2 1

Printed in the United States of America

For
Debbie and Toni

CONTENTS

ACKNOWLEDGMENTS

My friends Richard Kahlenberg, David Kolb, and Tom McGuire generously offered their insights and wisdom to my thinking about the book. I'm very grateful for their help. I would also like to thank David Pervin, who saw the light when others did not. And Toni—as always—gave beyond the call of duty.

—Tony Koltz

FOREWORD

by Tom Clancy

I first met Tony Zinni a couple of years ago at Quantico, Virginia, the famous Crossroads of the United States Marine Corps.

He's an intellectual product of Villanova University, and is therefore properly educated, and as a Marine four-star, he's a man who's been around the block more than once. I've gotten to know quite a few uniformed four-star officers. None of them have been anything other than bright students of human activity and history, one of my own hobbyhorses. To speak with one is rather like being in a graduate-level history seminar at Harvard or perhaps Oxford (I've spoken there once). If you ask such a person why the military does something in a certain way, you get a twenty minute lesson that goes back to Caius Julius Caesar, or maybe Alexander of Macedon, carries through past Agincourt, Normandy, and the Battle of the Bulge, with a stopover in Vietnam, and then you learn that *that* is the reason the Army or Marine Corps does it in *that* particular way. The lessons are always concise, logical, and illuminating.

General Zinni is a man who, with a decent book-learning education behind him, then learned to apply the lessons learned west of Philadelphia in the jungles of Vietnam, and later in every famous or infamous place on the globe. In the course of his post-college education, Zinni learned timeless and undying lessons in human behavior.

Not all cultures are the same, for one thing, and America in particular is a "special case" of all human activity. Warfare is ever a case of human behavior, which is a product of culture and history, including the sort that often is not actually written down. But in this book, Tony does some of the writing, allowing the reader to look at the world in a new and vital way, to see the world through the eyes of a professional warrior.

A warrior is different from the rest of us. People like myself perceive the world as a place in which to do business and make money; Tony looks at it as one who must just first of all survive the intricacies of life in a very different set of circumstances. Not better or worse than what we Americans are raised in, but *different* in many or even, in some cases, almost every way. We must learn how to do business with these people, to learn from them and also to teach them how to live in a world that is largely defined by American values and methods that the world might respect, but of which the world is also skeptical and suspicious.

In literature we often talk about the dichotomy between perception and reality, but in the real world perception often becomes reality. A belief is not the same thing as a fact, but a belief defines how people perceive facts. A person a hundred years ago would not have known what a helicopter is even if one had landed in his front yard. Today some people's reality is a belief system based on the writings of the Prophet Mohammed. Those beliefs are not, as a matter of fact, very different from Judaism and Christianity, at least not as they are written down, but cultural and other factors can make it seem that Muslims are our national enemies, when, as a matter of written fact, there is no such need for this to be.

What Tony has given us in this admirably clear and well thought out volume is the compilation of a bright man's journey around the world, all of which while wearing the prestigious uniform of our most elite military service. Tony Zinni is *all* Marine. Once I joked to him that when he cuts himself while shaving he bleeds green. He replied, "No, camouflage."

But Tony is also all American in his outlook, always looking for facts and answers to questions that he had to learn how to ask beforehand. At the four-star level, a warrior becomes a diplomat, dealing with citizens of other countries ranging from private soldiers to presidents, all of whom have different outlooks in terms of context or scale. A general officer must be able to speak with, learn from, and reason with such people not only in the pursuit of American national goals, but also in terms that can bring peace and reason to that particular part of the world. Tony is a man with what John Paul Jones once called "the nicest sense of personal honor." The word "integrity" has a special, almost mystical sense of meaning in the Marine Corps, and as a result of that, Tony has taught ethics at the university level—and I often wondered what it might be like to sit in those classes. Anywhere you go in the world, honesty is something that all men respect, and I have no doubt that General Zinni was an effective diplomat while wearing his well worn Marine utilities.

This book ought to be required reading for those who seek to serve our country's national interests. While not everyone will agree with everything written here, the overlying message is to keep your eyes and ears open, never to lose sight of our national goals, and above all to be faithful to our principles. You dance with the one who brung you, and Tony is a true patriot who understands the principles on which our country has been built. He's the son of an Italian immigrant who served his country in World War One, and ended up a junior NCO. I wish I could have met him. World War One was nobody's picnic, but that Zinni did his job well, and then taught his kids how to do it right. That background is the foundation of Tony's character, and it's served this friend of mine very well indeed.

—Tom Clancy 1–21–06

THE
BATTLE
FOR
PEACE

CHAPTER ONE

AMERICA'S POWER & PURPOSE

I look forward to a great future for America—a future in which our country will match its military strength with our moral restraint, its wealth with our wisdom, its power with our purpose.
—John F. Kennedy, 1963

America is great because she is good, but if America ever ceases to be good, America will cease to be great.
—Alexis de Tocqueville, 1835

The last assignment in my four-decade military career was to command the U.S. Central Command (CENTCOM), where I had responsibility for all military activities in a volatile area that included twenty-five countries—in East Africa, the Middle East, Southwest Asia, and Central Asia. For many years this region has occupied the red-hot center of what is often called the Arc of Instability or the Zone of Conflict—a belt stretching around the midsection of the earth containing the world's most turbulent, troubled, and unstable nations. Over the years of my military career, and later as a diplomat and businessman, I have spent considerable time in nearly every nation in the Zone of Conflict; I have developed a deep personal interest in each of them; and I have made many friends and close personal connections in those nations. I know the area well.

Immediately after 9/11, I received a flood of letters, emails, and calls from friends all over the world expressing condolence, shock, and anger over the horrific acts of that day. But one Arab friend was more than just upset by the shocking terrorist attacks; he seemed intensely worried about something deeper. And that caught my attention.

"I understand your sadness and your compassion," I told him, as we talked on the phone. "That's obvious. But I'm very interested in what's bothering you beyond that."

"I'm worried that this tragedy could cause America to stop being America," he said.

I asked him to explain.

"You Americans don't know your power, your influence, and your goodness," he said. "Your anger and the retaliation you're about to take are justified. But in doing what you must do to respond to this evil, I hope, for the sake of the world, that you never lose sight of your values and your sense of justice in the actions that you take. The world needs you more than you realize."

My friend was telling me much more than the obvious—that we Americans don't know our own power and influence. He was telling me that we haven't really learned how to use them to get what we want or need; that we don't really know who we are, in the sense that we've had to struggle to work out our proper role in today's world; and that our role must include the moral dimension that has been essential to America's actions in the world since the days of the nation's founders. This does not mean that America has always acted well, only that the attempt to act well has consistently guided us. What he was saying is that America always sought to do right—and that both our friends and our enemies have seen that.

It's tough to operate within a set of principles when the other guy does not; but that has always been our strength.

But my friend was probing even deeper, implicitly asking powerful and hard questions about America's totally new and unprecedented situation after the end of the Cold War. America is now the last superpower standing, the most powerful nation in the history of the planet by staggering orders of magnitude, and is capable of projecting every dimension of power and influence anywhere on earth. The direction that all of the earth's peoples will take over the next century will largely be determined by the United States' choices.

We have to lead. We have no choice. We're the 800-pound gorilla in an eight-by-ten room. We may not like being in that position, and we may wish we didn't make everybody else in the room nervous—when we move, the whole room knows it. But we can't help being who we are; and we can't help it that hardly anything goes on in the room that we don't affect.

That is what I believe former Secretary of State Madeleine Albright meant when she observed that the United States is "the indispensable nation." This was by no means an arrogant declaration; it was a statement of reality. We are the single nation that can make or break significant worldwide actions or international programs. People both inside and outside this country may not like this truth, but they know it's true. Everywhere I travel throughout the world, I get this from my friends: "Without you," they tell me, "we can't make it happen."

There will be no Middle East peace without United States participation in the peace process. There will be no global environmental policy without U.S. participation. There will be no global health policy. No global economic and trade policy. And without the United States, you can forget the United Nations.

The catch is, our choices are anything but clear. What does world leadership mean in the post–Cold War environment? Nobody knows. Nobody has been there before. There are no models.

Debates on this question have been fierce within the last three administrations . . . and without resolution.

Are we the world's policeman? Are we an empire? How do we choose our priorities for acting in the world when we can't do everything? What are the limits of our power? What are the limits of our actions? What are the limits of our influence? What are the limits of our leadership? How much can we demand, and of whom? What freedoms and responsibilities does our supreme position give us that other First World players don't possess? How do we work with and within international organizations?

The very asking of these questions—and there are many others like them—indicates the extent of our confusion.

THE AMERICAN EMPIRE

My answer to questions about America's role will make some Americans—and many non-Americans—uncomfortable: *We are an empire,* and empires have a nasty reputation. Yet no other word covers the preeminent position America has achieved in the world. That's what it means to be "the indispensable nation," the only nation whose power and influence are felt everywhere in the world. Never before in the history of humankind has a nation been in this position—the world's sole remaining empire, yet a very different breed of empire from all the other empires that have risen and collapsed over the course of history.

Traditionally, empires are born through military conquest, and military power provides the basis of their influence. Empires take over and administer territories; they send out troops to occupy them and oversee security; they send out governors and managers; they exploit natural resources and labor and extract the wealth of the occupied lands on behalf of the empire's core. They command and dictate.

That kind of empire is dead (though it could conceivably come alive again). America is not an empire of conquest and self-interest, though some accuse us of that ("All you Americans want is to grab

Iraq's oil"); and the source of our influence goes way beyond our military power. Yet America is an empire that cannot command or dictate, and does not want to; it can only influence. It is not an empire of conquest; it's an empire of influence.

The President of the United States has announced to the world that the United States intends to make the world democratic; that we are going to make the world operate on market economies; that we will promote and protect human rights; and that we will use all elements of our power to make that happen. . . . In essence, *we* decide how *you* shape your society.

I don't know what to call a statement like that other than an imperial pronouncement.

I'm not saying our nation is wrong to set these goals. I like them. We obviously feel that the goals are right and good and morally correct. But they reflect *our* morals and beliefs.

That's imperialism. Not imperialism at the point of a bayonet, but imperialism achieved through the other dimensions of power— our unmatched ability to collect and disseminate information, our leadership in diplomacy, our vast resources, our social and cultural influence, our economic influence, our moral influence, and our military might.

These touch everyone in the world, sometimes directly and forcefully (we invaded Iraq and easily toppled the Saddam Hussein regime), sometimes more subtly. Everyone listens to American music. Everyone watches American movies. Everyone eats American food. Everyone wears American fashions. There's hardly anyone out there who does not look out at the world through American lenses. Even those who hate us perceive their world by reference to American culture, values, and power.

During my visits to the Middle East, people have kidded me, "Hey there's the American Cultural Center."

"The American Cultural Center?"

"McDonald's, Burger King, KFC."

And yet, for all our matchless power, capable of touching any point on the globe with every dimension of power—no other nation on the planet matches us in even one of those dimensions—we are not accomplishing the goals in the world that most matter to us: enhancing democracy and respect for human rights, giving people opportunities to improve their lives, and increasing the security and stability that are the necessary foundations for those happy outcomes. Often we don't know how to wield our power and influence; where to wield our power; or even the scope of our power. We would like a secure peace in the world. Yet we are unsure of the actions needed to achieve it.

The failure begins at home.

AMERICA'S PURPOSE

Our nation's leaders—skilled, experienced, dedicated people in three administrations—have struggled to adapt to the radical and dangerous worldwide seismic shift that followed the Cold War . . . with success that's at best mixed.

The first Bush administration put together, under a UN resolution, the remarkable international coalition that fought the first Gulf War, and in doing so created an effective and lasting model for dealing with complex problems and crises. After the fall of the Soviet empire, the administration was forward-looking in its attempts (organized by Secretary of State James Baker and Ambassador Richard Armitage) to connect peacefully with the new nations that once made up the Soviet Union and to lead an international coalition aimed at launching a new Marshall Plan to help these nations get on their feet. Sadly, their grand dream died in the euphoria that followed the collapse of the Soviet military threat.

On the downside, the administration was naïve in its assumptions about the changes brought on by the end of the Soviet threat. They didn't grasp the new world environment and accepted uncritically their own slogans proclaiming an automatic "New World Order" and a "Peace Dividend." After the euphoria died, we discovered that we had neither.

The Clinton administration's multilateral and multifaceted approach to world trouble-spots was an excellent initiative to reshape the world in a positive way, but the administration never came up with the energy, organization, or resources needed to match the words.

The second Bush administration has promoted a strong, noble, and positive sense of values—human rights, freedom, democracy—and is willing to commit energy and resources to this cause. Yet its aggressive, unilateral approach has alienated the international community and blocked the international cooperation necessary for achieving these goals. The clearest example of the second Bush administration's unilateral approach is the invasion and occupation of Iraq. But not far behind is their resistance and hostility to a number of treaties with broad international support.

Each of the three post–Cold War administrations has had real accomplishments. Yet, they have all failed

- to fully grasp the meaning of the post–Cold War changes and to devise a coherent, integrated strategy for them;
- to see the signs of critical instability emerging from the post–Cold War environment or to grasp its underlying causes;
- to confront developing trouble until it has degenerated into a violent confrontation, that is, until it has turned into a crisis;
- to develop tools other than military force for managing the crisis (and when that hasn't proven practical, the crisis has been left to simmer—or grow worse);
- to implement, enforce, and sustain peace, order, and stability once the crisis appears to be settled;

- to commit the time and resources necessary to accomplish genuine reconstruction and restoration of a stable society—or to even seriously attempt it;
- and to reorganize our outdated governmental structure to better integrate the elements of power needed to deal with today's threats and requirements.

We have seen the effects of these failures again and again—in Afghanistan in the 1980s, in Somalia and the former Yugoslavia in the 1990s, in Iraq and Afghanistan today, and in many simmering crises in Africa, the Middle East, Latin America, and Asia.

Why did our leaders fail? Because they were incompetent? Because they were foolish? Because they were blind?

Hardly. They failed primarily because they were working within a governmental system, organizational structure, and national strategy that had served admirably and successfully during the fifty years of Cold War but had not evolved to adapt to the changes that swept in after its collapse.

Critics have accused Presidents Clinton and Bush of failing to make the correct strategic decisions to stop Al Qaeda and perhaps prevent the 9/11 attacks. Such criticisms are unfair to both presidents. They depended on outdated organizations and systems that failed to sense the changes in the world and to present an integrated view of the threat and the necessary responses. As the 9/11 Commission reported, good men and women were working within an antiquated process.

Later, we had a war plan for Iraq but not a plan to reconstruct and win the peace. We had a military organization that could defeat the enemy but not an organization that could reconstruct the society.

Our nation has time and again confronted the disorder and crises that instabilities and conflicts produce. Yet we have been inconsistent and haphazard in how we have chosen to accomplish our goals—both in our basic principles and in subsequent actions.

Some of that is for good, practical reasons: "Here I can make a difference. Here I can't."

But some of it comes from our failure to engage in basic strategic thinking. The two world wars of the past century were followed by worldwide seismic shifts as powerful as the one that followed the Cold War. The lesson each time has been the same: the world cannot find peace and stability by sailing on its own rudderless course. There has to be a map, a direction, to guide us through the confusing and dangerous new world environment. We need an overarching strategy to deal coherently with threatening, unstable parts of the world . . . a national security strategy that redefines our role in the new century, defines our goals, and shapes our national organizations to achieve those goals.

A new statement of national strategy will take into account the challenges presented by the reordered world that has followed the end of the Cold War.

It will derive from our strongly held values and principles, and from the level of security and well-being we want to ensure both for ourselves and for others—essentially peace, stability, and prosperity; it will take into account the availability of our resources and our strongly held priorities for using them; it will come with a new, comprehensive analysis of the environment that we're faced with—the challenges, the threats, the issues, the potential pitfalls; and it will redefine our role in the world—who we are, what we expect of ourselves, and what we're willing to do. The new strategy will acknowledge that we can't do everything. Some threats can at best be contained. Some we can't deal with at all. Some we *must* deal with.

Our starting point must be the actual condition of the world. What's out there?

We have to look at the world in nitty-gritty detail—nations, regions, trends, problems, unstable situations, emerging crises, conflicts. We have to analyze, synthesize, and understand . . . as best we can. Out of this should come a *realistic* vision that answers these questions: What kind of world do we want? Where do our interests lie? What threatens us? What can we do about that? What's the best we can achieve? How can we get there? What stands in our way? . . . What are we doing to ourselves that stands in our way?

The process of vision making does not stop with goals and ends. It goes on to determine the ways and means available to achieve them. The strategy is not the grand finale, it is the lens through which we must look at our actions in the world. It directs and guides them. Actions in the world that don't derive from our strategic vision risk being at best improvised and ad hoc, and at worst mindless.

Strategy must lead directly to actions.

We can look at this overall process from world to strategy and back to the world as an arc—I'll call it an "arc of action." We start with the real world and its threats and challenges; we move back to a strategic vision, setting goals for dealing with these threats and challenges and devising ways to achieve the goals; and then we return to the nitty-gritty actions we must take in the real world to minimize the threats and diminish the challenges.

We'll find this process—or this arc—working at every level of society. Strategy building takes place in families as well as in nation-states.

A well-functioning family will have a strategic vision, with strategic goals that might include a better home, college for the kids, adequate healthcare, and a happy and fruitful retirement. But it's not enough to have a strategic vision. The family has to make it happen. And they will have to start from the actual conditions they face and the resources they expect to have available.

THE EVOLUTION OF AMERICA'S PURPOSE

As we look back over our history, we can clearly see how America's strategic vision—its national purpose—emerged at each stage of our development and how this purpose was commonly understood and accepted by the people and their governments.

In the first decades of our national existence, we focused on structuring our form of governance and the interaction among the states. In that period our purpose was to lay the foundation for a remarkable experiment in the construction of human society and in the definition of core values in the context of this bold new concept.

The years of birth were followed by a long era of expansion and growth. During this period, we pushed out to our continental and hemispheric bounds, while remaining deliberately isolated from the problems plaguing the rest of the world. Our purpose was clear— Manifest Destiny—the fullest expansion of our national borders and the defense of our hemisphere from the imperial probes of outside powers hungry to reestablish the evils of colonial dominance that we had fought off at our nation's birth.

After resolving the unfinished internal problems that divided our nation during the nineteenth century, we began in the twentieth century to reach out from our self-imposed isolation. The war with Spain, Teddy Roosevelt's Great White Fleet, and Woodrow Wilson's decision to intervene in World War I marked the first American forays onto the international scene. These were daring steps for a nation that had turned its previous purposes into reality and now stood poised to play a significant role in the world it had long kept at arm's length.

These early steps proved to be too daring, as it turned out. America looked out at the new world horizon, covered her eyes, and backed off.

Wilson's dream of a new world expressed in his Fourteen Points and his desire for us to join the League of Nations was too bold for a Congress and a nation still wary of "foreign entanglements." We retreated into isolation and failed to move toward a new national purpose that might have changed the course of a world headed to a repeat of the tragically misnamed "war to end all wars."

December 7, 1941, ended forever America's isolation. It thrust America into the global role we had resisted for a century and a half.

The attack on Pearl Harbor sparked an acceleration in the development of our power and influence that eventually made us the world's sole superpower.

During the era stretching from the onset of World War II to the fall of the Soviet Union, our role and purpose was to defend and deter—as the protector of the free world. We stood as the standard and bulwark around which all those threatened by evil ideologies and rapacious conquerors could rally. We were the shining beacon, the model of noble values and principles.

From the beginning of our national existence until the fall of the Soviet Union, we were reluctant interventionists. We were defenders, not attackers. We did what we had to do when threatened or attacked, but we did not seek to impose change. We wanted to remain Jefferson's beacon, an example to follow. We did not want to become crusaders.

Today—even at this moment of unchallenged power—we are faced with a new and previously unknown kind of world. Our borders are no longer impenetrable. Isolation is no longer tenable. Even a defensive posture is no longer tenable. A national purpose rooted in isolation won't work today. It's not enough to be the shining beacon.

September 11, like December 7, has made it clear that we can't ignore this new, more dangerous world. This world demands a new national purpose—a purpose based on the premise that we all prosper in a peaceful and stable world and that we all lose in an unstable world. It is no longer a zero-sum game. In the era of imperialism and colonialism, nations and societies gained at the expense of others. That is no longer the case. If the powerful fleece the weak, the resulting instability will breed the problems that will come to plague the powerful.

We have no choice now. We must be active and engaged in the world. This doesn't mean we should impose our will to effect change, unless we are directly threatened. It does mean we need to deftly use all our elements of power in an integrated and intelligent manner to generate stability in parts of the world where the myriad problems we face have their roots. And to the same end, we must use our leadership position to create international cooperation and participation.

The arc of action that leads from the world to a vision of national purpose and then back to actions in the world begins, of course, in the world.

CHAPTER TWO

IN THE FOXHOLE

Commanders should be counseled, chiefly, by persons of known talent; by those whose knowledge is gained from experience; by those who are present at the scene of action, who see the country, who see the enemy; who see the advantages that occasions offer, and who, like people embarked on the same ship, are sharers of the danger. If, therefore, anyone thinks himself qualified to give advice respecting the war which I am to conduct, let him come with me to Macedonia.

—Lucius Amelius Paulus, circa 172 B.C.

The world outside the United States is a diverse and multidimensional environment, rich in peoples, cultures, languages, religions, sensibilities, and sensitivities. Few Americans directly experience that richness. Fewer still immerse themselves in it. Yet a major part of the understanding necessary to create a national strategic vision requires not just the experience of the richness beyond our borders, but a deep understanding based on long immersion out there. The same understanding of what's out there is needed at the other end of the arc, where actions are taken. The importance of this kind of understanding first started to become clear to me many decades ago.

In 1967, I stepped for the first time into an environment radically alien to the Philadelphia where I grew up: Vietnam. My assignment there—as our Marine Corps' most junior adviser to the elite

Vietnamese Marines—launched a decades-long, event-filled, mind-opening journey through dozens of no less alien environments.

When I arrived on Easter morning in March I was a naïve, impressionable, twenty-two-year-old second lieutenant. Infantry officers like me all knew that war is about going out and killing the enemy and winning battles. That's war. That's success.

But my assignment as adviser showed me a very different view of this war—and of all wars. I lived with the Vietnamese in the field and in the villages; I spoke Vietnamese; I was immersed in their culture; I hardly saw another American.

From this perspective, I saw that military success on the battlefield alone was not going to give us ultimate victory. I saw, as did my contemporaries, the courage and sacrifice of our troops. Yet I also saw how civil society was reacting to the conflict; I saw failures in the side we were supporting; I saw corruption and incompetence there; I saw little progress in building a viable nation. And I saw how we were convincing ourselves that we were building hope and promise in the Vietnamese people while the people were seeing themselves as caught between two stones. When I came back home, I realized that the war I had experienced was a different war than most Americans were seeing. I'd seen the war through a vastly different lens. We correctly advertised that to win this conflict, we needed to win the hearts and minds of the people; but on the ground, it seemed to be all about body counts. Our strategic objectives seemed right to me—I thought then and I still think it was a war worth fighting—but our attrition-based execution on the ground didn't match our objectives.

How did I come to these realizations?

In Vietnam, I passed through a series of powerful experiences that I later realized were hinge moments in my life. Though I didn't necessarily know it then, these were turning points that started me on the road that eventually led me to the thoughts reflected in these pages.

We can start with the Marine Corps' approach to the adviser's role . . . very different from the way others did it. Links between

South Vietnamese and American forces were obviously necessary, both for the sake of coordination and to help provide the South Vietnamese with the military, technological, and logistical support they couldn't provide for themselves. To achieve that end, most other advisory efforts were built around teams of seven or eight soldiers and officers who stayed together as a unit in the field, often separate from the Vietnamese units they were supposed to be advising. In some cases teams left their Vietnamese units at nightfall, leaving them to their own devices when they were most vulnerable. It was a case of American unwillingness to trust the Vietnamese and to totally immerse advisers in the culture. That was risky.

The Marine Advisory Unit was created along very different lines. A remarkable old Marine colonel named Victor Croizat, with years of experience in the country, had a better idea. Croizat was a French speaker sent as an observer to work with the French during the Indochina War. Later, he was left to work with the South Vietnamese navy and a fledgling river assault group that was the embryonic Vietnamese Marine Corps. Later still, when the decision was made to create a Marine Advisory Unit for Vietnam, Croizat said, "If we want to be effective, we've got to be totally absorbed into the Vietnamese units, totally dependent on them—no teams. We'll put an officer or two in a battalion, and that's it. Our radio operators will be Vietnamese. Our 'cowboys' (batmen) will be Vietnamese. We'll learn their language, wear their uniforms, completely immerse ourselves in their customs, traditions, and style of fighting.

"That way we'll gain trust. And we'll really see the fighting as they see it, which is the best way to support and advise them." The side benefit, of course, was how much more we advisers would learn from this approach.

And so the Marine advisers got thrown into Vietnam; and we were *there*.

The Vietnamese Marines were not at all like the larger ARVN (Army of the Republic of Vietnam) units. They were a small, very elite, very tough, light infantry unit—incredibly capable in the kinds of engagements they were formed to fight. Unlike our own military, they didn't normally operate apart from civil society but lived off the land and slept in the villages. We shared all that with them. We started to look at the war through their eyes. This gave us a depth of understanding of them, of the Vietnamese people, and of the war that allowed us to be more effective in our advice and support. After a while we began to think, dress, and even look like them.

It soon hit me that I was fighting with a unit who saw this war in the long term. They were not impatient, like Americans, to end this war *right now.* Their tour wasn't for a year, the way it was for our troops. No one was promising to "have them home by Christmas," as our political leaders were ridiculously vowing. They didn't bounce in and out as we did, thinking: "It's my duty to make a difference and bring this to a decisive battle *right now.*" For Americans, refusing battle was out of the question. But so was looking at the war in a longer term context, as they—and the enemy—did.

The enemy avoided decisive battles unless he had a clear advantage. He wanted to give you the death of a thousand cuts over many years. He only wanted to fight on his terms and when he had the advantage. The South Vietnamese Marines understood that context. It was their context.

One day we had a chance to follow an enemy unit into the bush; I wanted to charge forward and engage them (risking a trap). But the battalion commander nixed that idea. "We can't rush headlong into battle," he counseled. "It's not a question of courage or cowardice, but of short-term gains versus long-term gains. I'm going to fight on my terms, not his. I'll see that guy again tomorrow." He did.

The complexities and paradoxes I was seeing in that war came into sharp focus for me one evening in the summer of '67. This quiet and peaceful moment—all too short—burned deep into my memory. It profoundly changed my life, though I was far from aware of that then.

At that time we were operating in northern II Corps: I was enjoying a friendly conversation with the family of a village chief, whose house I was sharing, in fiercely contested Binh Dinh province. The evening was pleasantly cool, and we were sitting outside after a tasty meal.

"Do you have any pictures of your family in the USA?" the chief's wife, an elderly lady, asked.

I pulled out what I had—a picture of my wife and me in front of her parents' home. The old lady stared at it, shook her head, and then looked up at me with a deeply penetrating expression.

"Why are you here in Vietnam?" she asked me.

I gave her the standard answer about stopping communism and protecting democracy and our Vietnamese allies.

"But what are you going to do to change things there?" she asked, her hand pointing toward the south.

I thought she had made a mistake—the enemy was to the north. Then I realized she was saying exactly what she meant to say: The corrupt South Vietnamese government that lurched from coup to coup, replacing one general with another, was as much an enemy to her as the Vietcong and the infiltrators from the north.

But that was far from the full force of what she was telling me. She was not asking us to go fix the government in Saigon because they were, in her eyes, just as bad as the Vietcong and North Vietnamese and offered nothing for ordinary people like her. Her point was this: "You want me and my children to fight and die for a cause; but the cause you are giving me to fight and die for is not anything I *can* fight and die for." She saw herself as a victimized third party, caught between forces she could not control. We were promising some vague future hope of democracy and well-being. She needed immediate security and assurance of survival.

We Americans had a cause to fight for: we were going to block communism and promote democracy. We were going to prop up dominoes: stop the communists in South Vietnam before they toppled the rest of Southeast Asia. Our value system and reasons for being in Vietnam were very clear to us—at least in the beginning.

We had a naïve belief that the Vietnamese people had one big choice: They could be either good or bad. They could follow either freedom or communism. We were projecting our way of thinking onto them.

But the people were taking a third course: "A pox on both your houses. Which of you is helping me right now? Don't give me your idealistic rhetoric, when I can't get food on my table or step out of my house without getting shot at by one side or the other." What they were fighting for was in no way clear to them.

My comrades in our military went over there with the idea that we and the South Vietnamese were all fighting together in the same war for the same reasons with the same aims. The answer was "yes" to much of that. But not to all of that. When you intervene in a civil war, you are still the outsider, you are still the alien. You are coming into a different culture.

Meanwhile, the lens through which most of my counterparts looked at the Vietnamese clouded their ability to see the subtle realities that made *all* the difference.

This was a war where there were no front lines. Americans had to look at every Vietnamese with suspicion: Is the barber at the local base a Vietcong? Is the lady who washes your clothes a Vietcong? Who laid that mine on the street that killed my buddy? Those villagers had to know it was there. How come they didn't tell us?

Those kinds of things were very difficult for many U.S. soldiers to understand. They were thinking: "We're here risking our lives to bring these people freedom. Why don't they support us?"

What those soldiers didn't understand was the burden of fear those people were carrying . . . or their levels of sympathy for or apathy toward the other side (which didn't necessarily mean they accepted the other side's imposition of their way of life) . . . or the levels of intimidation practiced by the other side ("why should I lay it on the line out here and get killed?") . . . or some of the other activities going on in the villages at night when Americans weren't there. But I did. Not because I was any more brilliant or insightful than my contemporaries. I certainly was not. I was thrown into the deep end of this highly complex environment feet first and exposed to all its complexity.

Americans were outsiders.

The same thing is happening right now in Iraq. I have seen it in Somalia, where the clan loyalty was a stronger influence than what we offered. I saw it again in Aceh in Sumatra, where separatist rebels have been fighting the Indonesian government for years. I saw it again in Mindanao, where the Moros have been fighting the Philippine government for decades. I saw it among the Palestinian people. The ordinary people say, "To hell with both of you."

That's what we'd missed in Vietnam. We were saying to the people: "These are the goals. We want to bring you democracy, freedom, self-determination, prosperity." But the means to that—the government we set up in Saigon—was not a government they could die for. We needed to stop the spread of communism. They needed to survive.

It was not enough to give them rhetoric or ideology; we had to offer them a path to a goal that would empower them—a goal they could believe in, one that would meet immediate, tangible, and pressing needs . . . and one that was worth dying for. And we weren't doing that. For the first time, it was hitting me that victory required more than most Americans imagined and that war had dimensions beyond winning battles and counting dead enemies. It's not enough to win battles: the people have to back your cause. The ordinary people, civil society, were the center of gravity, the key to victory.

The other thing I learned in Vietnam, and would relearn in many more places, was the importance of understanding the culture. There are thousands of cultures in the world and thousands of languages. Some things don't translate, even though we can clearly recognize their logic and goodness from our own cultural perspective. Those hundreds of cultures have been shaped and forged by centuries of history, by the physical environment, and by their evolving traditions and belief systems. If you want to change a society or influence its direction and choices, you must do it with an understanding of its culture, within the context of its culture, and with an understanding of the plight of its people. Years later I would reflect on a lesson learned, from many experiences around the world, regarding cultural intelligence. To me this was a necessary ingredient for planning the numerous military interventions we undertook, yet it always seemed missing.

My insight that evening in Binh Dinh province might be called an epiphany—some kind of road to Damascus moment. But it did not hit me that way at the time; I didn't see a flash of total understanding. In my view, great epiphanies are rare. For me, there may come an awakening, like that one, and then later maybe a glimpse at something deeper, and later other glimpses. And then I gradually have a realization that causes me to look back over the awakening and the glimpses and try to grasp it all in the light of the realization. I constantly reexamine. I'm still looking back and learning from Vietnam.

As I reexamine the chain of experiences, I might be able to pinpoint where it began. But there was never a flash-bang where I suddenly had full understanding.

In Vietnam most of my contemporaries saw a single dimension of war: kill and defeat the enemy—attrition warfare. At the same time, I was going through the first gleam of awakening that there had to be more than a totally military solution to this conflict. I was beginning to see political, economic, social, ethnic, cultural, religious, and many other complicated dimensions and puzzling factors that made up this conflict.

I returned for a second tour of duty in Vietnam, commanding a U.S. Marine infantry company, and saw these perspectives firsthand. My view of this conflict became far more complex than the simple military dimension.

My immersion in Vietnam was followed by many other immersions in many other nations and cultures. In my military service—and later as a leader in humanitarian relief operations, diplomat, international businessman, and academic—I've worked in more than seventy countries. In time, interacting with other cultures turned into a natural fit. I'm fascinated by cultures—by the complex ways history and geography have molded people into whatever they have become and by how they have evolved a different view of the world than ours.

I learned over time that from society to society there's little difference in fundamental values and fundamental concerns. But there are great differences in approaches to these values and concerns. We all value family. We all value life. We all value keeping our word. But our approaches to expressing these values and prioritizing them can be remarkably different. We don't have different values, but we shape our approaches to these values in all kinds of different ways. And these differences become issues that spark misunderstandings . . . and sometimes spark conflicts.

Plunging into alien environments is one of my passions; it gives me enormous pleasure, but it is not just a pleasant pastime.

We Americans no longer have the luxury of existing as a nation isolated from the rest of the world. The barriers we trusted through our history to prevent contamination from the outside have collapsed as permanently as the Berlin Wall. We now have no choice but to engage with the many different peoples out there in all their many dimensions; and we can't do this as outsiders, looking at them through our own lenses, trying to force our own thinking on them— as we did in Vietnam, as we are doing today in Iraq.

This is the great lesson my decades out there on the pointy end of the spear have taught me. This is the unique perspective open to those on the front lines of both warmaking and peacemaking. This is "the foxhole view."

On the face of it, a foxhole offers a limited angle of vision. Even though it places you deep inside the center of the action, you don't see very much from there, or very far. But think about it. Seeing the action from several hundred foxholes all over the world over many years can produce a cumulative experience that's hard to beat. And if you've not only been in foxholes but have also sipped tea with leaders, met with shopkeepers, walked the streets and talked to ordinary people, eaten meals with businessmen and military and political leaders around the world; if you've both studied the history of those people and walked the ground in their villages where the history was made; and if in your conversations you've begun to understand how the history and geography viscerally affects the people . . . then the knowledge gained from foxholes might start to prove enlightening. You might start to see what's going on out there in ways that people who lack your experience may fail to see.

The foxhole view is not just a military perspective. Many others who labor in the fields—diplomats, aid workers, journalists—also experience the reality on the ground and the frequent disconnects between policies back home and that reality. Being there gives them the sights, sounds, smells, the sense of the raw emotions, and the appreciation for the complex environment rarely known by policymakers far removed from the scene.

Even then, you can't depend on the foxhole experience to bring wisdom.

"You've led many military campaigns," somebody allegedly said to Frederick the Great, one of history's outstanding military commanders. "And you've fought many battles. Who is the most experienced member of your military?"

"See that mule over there?" Frederick said, pointing. "That mule made every one of my campaigns and was in every battle, but in the end he's still a jackass."

Whether the story is true or not, its message is true. Experiences alone are not enough. It's not enough to have been there. It's how well we see deep inside and draw understanding out of the experiences. It's extracting the important elements that provides a deeper appreciation for all the dimensions of what's going on. And then it's using all that as the basis for making wise decisions.

This front-line perspective is not gained by the "touch and gos" of "airport strategists"—Washington political leaders who drop in for a day or two, get the VIP bubble around them, receive the dazzling PowerPoint briefs, cherry-pick facts that support their preconceived and stated positions and theories, and then return home claiming to have "been there" and validated their brilliance.

Experienced military commanders who have seen action at many levels know that the picture of the battle in the command post can be very different from the view from the foxhole. They know that a top-down system—one totally driven by the command post—will not work. In the command post you have the advantage of seeing the "big picture" and of making calculated decisions apart from the chaos and confusion of the close fight. At the command post you can bring together all the information, considerations, and resources to develop courses of action. But you also need that sense of the battle that comes only from the front lines. It's at the front lines where the effects of actions, decisions, and events are most evident; where opportunity and calamity can be most clearly perceived; where factors unknown to higher echelons can be detected. In the command post, commanders and planners can fall into the trap of falling in love with their plan. (I always cautioned my staff against that trap.) It can cause them to select only the facts that support the plan that they have a vested interest in promoting—or that they simply hope will succeed—and to be blind to all the signs that the plan is flawed or is failing, or that opportunities are presenting themselves that warrant a new course of action.

This is not an either/or situation—front lines versus command posts. The ideal is to blend the careful analysis of the command post with the on-the-scene assessment from the front. The ideal is a system that works both ways—up and down—and is built on trust and open exchange.

Why didn't the strategists and theorists who framed our policies during Vietnam see what a second lieutenant had thrust in front of him? Why do we often find in our policymakers an intellectual arrogance that dismisses the input from the field?

❧

Flash forward to February 11, 2003, a few weeks before we launched the Iraq war.

I had been called before the Senate Foreign Relations Committee to give my views on the coming war. As I waited to be questioned, I listened to the testimony from the panel in front of me—planners from the State and Defense Departments.

"Planners?" I thought with horror as I listened to them. "The planners have no plan. They're not thinking about what comes after we've invaded Iraq and taken Baghdad. Defeating the Republican Guard and taking the capital are what would traditionally define victory. But are the planners considering the complexities that go far beyond that?"

This was coming on top of what I'd already heard a few days earlier when the secretary of defense had announced that the original plan he had been presented was "old and stale." The plan he was referring to had been generated by CENTCOM. I had spent several years at CENTCOM, three of them as commander. I knew that plan and the ten years of planning and assessment that had gone into it by people who were actually familiar with Iraq and the region. It was a living plan. It not only took into account defeating Iraq's military forces, it took into account the aftermath.

I had also heard the secretary's deputy dispute the experienced Army chief of staff's estimate of the numbers of troops required. And I had heard interpretations of intelligence that many of us with deep experience in the region felt were far off the mark from the true threat.

Later, as the war did not progress as advertised, I heard the secretary of defense dismiss failures that had clearly resulted from poor or nonexistent planning by tossing off snappy quips ("stuff happens") or by quoting old military axioms ("No plan survives contact with the enemy"). Yet he had failed to grasp another military principle best expressed by General Dwight D. Eisenhower: "In preparing for battle I have always found that plans are useless, but planning is indispensable."

Why was the Washington view so different from what we who had lived in and experienced this region for a decade saw and understood to be true?

"These so-called planners," I thought, "see the invasion of Iraq through their own narrow simplistic lens. They're thinking: 'The transformation of Iraq into a modern, democratic, capitalist society couldn't be easier: Once we've popped the cork and taken out Saddam, we're going to be welcomed with flowers in the streets. And then Iraq will self-order.'"

I knew they weren't seeing the aftermath.

"In my experience," I thought, "that's going to be a lot more difficult, complex, and destabilizing than they imagine. Taking Baghdad and removing the regime won't end the conflict."

After I took my seat in front of the committee, I tried to make this point.

In an earlier question, Senator Norman Coleman, the junior senator from Minnesota, had implied that Iraq would clearly be a better place without Saddam Hussein. Of course removing Saddam would be a plus; but I had a worrisome feeling that the situation in Iraq could actually become worse in many respects than it was under Saddam if we didn't plan and provide for a whole host of complex political, economic, security, humanitarian, ethnic, religious, and other factors that could complicate our efforts to reconstruct the country. I didn't sense in what I was hearing any accounting for these factors or anything like that level of planning. Removing Saddam would not put Iraq on automatic pilot headed for stability.

"I want to address the issue of 'anything is better than what we have,'" I said. "Senator Coleman, I would say that we threw the Soviets out of Afghanistan with the idea that, Soviets out—got to be better than anything that can follow, and we left them with the Taliban eventually. So anyone who has to live in this region and has to stay there and protect our interests year in, year out, does not look at this as a start and end, as an exit strategy, as a two-year tenure. As long as you are going to have a U.S. Central Command, you are going to be out there and have to deal with whatever you put down on the ground."

I went on to explain to the committee not only the difficulty of what we were undertaking—reconstructing a nation with complex problems—but also how we would have to live with what we created or failed to create.

Starting a war unleashes a lot of kinetic energy. When you do that, you have to monitor that energy; you have to control it; you have to look hard at the effects you're going to generate in many different dimensions; and you have to look to the end result you want to achieve and how to get there. You also need to understand the costs and risks you face. When you pull the plug on a tyrant who controls all facets of life in a society, you have to be prepared to fill the vacuum. It doesn't neatly self-order. When you knock things out of balance, you've got to be prepared to put them back into balance; you have to know what it's going to take to put them back in balance. God knows what you're going to end up with if all you do is just launch the war and unleash the energy without thinking through these issues.

The warning from the foxhole is to take a deeper look at this world. Things are changing and we need to think through what those changes mean to us.

Senator Norm Coleman is an intelligent, well-informed, well-intentioned man. He wasn't wrong that Iraq would be better after Saddam Hussein, but I wanted to be sure the committee members understood that making Iraq better was not an automatic process. I felt that the committee had to understand that assumptions that seem logical from Washington may not turn out that way on the scene. It isn't that simple.

The issue is not that their intentions or the actions that follow from them are ill conceived. It's their lack of understanding of the complexity out there on the ground. They don't see what Clausewitz described as the "fog and friction" of war. They don't understand how this seemingly excellent cause can produce so many terrible effects . . . or how removing an evil tyrant—whose existence is a major cause of instability in the region—can unleash a chain of events that produces even more instability than he did.

After the first Gulf War, I took part as a young brigadier general in one of its messier aftermaths—the rescue of the Kurds, my first plunge into large-scale humanitarian relief. After their failed rebellion against Saddam Hussein, 500,000 Kurds had been driven out of their homeland in northern Iraq and were camped on the desolate, wintry mountain ridges along the Iraq-Turkey border. A gigantic humanitarian tragedy was in the making. Operation Provide Comfort (an international—though largely American—effort) saved thousands of lives.

Early in the operation, I got a call from the Joint Chiefs of Staff back in Washington. It was cold; we were in the middle of winter; and back in the United States TV clips were showing shivering Kurds as they wandered into the mountain camps. So the order came from the Director of the Joint Chiefs: "Drop blankets. Those people are freezing out there."

But the truth was that when the Kurds came into the camps, we had no problem warming them up and keeping them warm.

The big shortage was food and medicine. The priority was to get as much food and medicine as we could onto the pallets and into the bundles we were loading on our aircraft and airdropping. And that's what I told him.

But he said, "You will drop blankets."

So we had to repack the bundles and put in hundreds of blankets.

And predictably, when the bundles fell out of the sky, the Kurds tore them open and threw away the blankets. They were looking for the food and medicine.

But back here an image had created a mindset; the mindset had produced a stupid order . . . yet the order was made with the best of intentions. You can't accuse those who ordered us to drop blankets of being hard-hearted! In fact, when I thought about it, the decision would have seemed totally logical from Washington. Those blanket-strewn mountaintops I flew over many months after the airdrops continued to remind me of this.

The results, in this case, were more amusing than harmful. But the results of the soda-straw Washington view were not so benign following our invasion of Iraq in 2003; nor were they benign in Afghanistan after we pushed out the Soviets and left.

FOXHOLES AND WONKS

I can't claim to be a strategist or policy expert. But I can claim to have occupied many "foxholes" all over the world. I've stood on many front lines. I've learned many lessons out there . . . lessons, I've come to realize, that lead me to very different conclusions than I take from the analysis and policies coming out of the leading academic institutions, think tanks, intelligence centers, and policy shops back home. There, brilliant scholars, thinkers, and analysts logically process courses of action, based on the most credible and best informed intelligence. The perspectives that come from the top can't be discounted. On that level, there is a better sense of considerations we don't see on the front lines: political and diplomatic considerations that realistically have to be taken into account. They also have a broader perspective. They can see large-scale trends and developments—measures of population growth or decline, of wealth or poverty, health or disease, education or illiteracy, security or insecurity. They can see how there are limits on resources, stresses on the environment, and other broad priorities that you can't see from your position on the front.

Yet I have to keep asking myself: "What world are they thinking about? Is it the same world where I've stood on the front lines? *Do they have any real sense of that world?*"

Too many of our policymakers are products of an outdated spoils system rooted in the nineteenth century. The president has the authority to make over 3,000 appointments—from heads of important agencies to ambassadors to major countries. Too often presidents offer these big jobs to old college roommates, friends of golf partners, or political contributors—people who have none of the requisite skills or background to effectively handle these jobs. In the complex world environment we now face, we can no longer afford to have inexperienced political appointees in powerful and critical government positions. The aftermath of 2005's Hurricane Katrina, which blasted New Orleans and much of the southern gulf states, should tell us that this system of spoils has to be abolished.

Few on the front lines are personally invested in strategies and policies they themselves designed or supported, or in the administrations that produced them. These are operational people, not theorists. Their interest is in taking actions, not taking positions. They want to make the actions come out right. Selectively citing or spinning facts to promote a self-serving position hardly ever enters their minds. They cringe at the stream of sound-bite strategies that flow from the Washington politicians and wonks who stay on message despite the facts on the ground that give the lie to the courses they advocate.

Unfortunately, the makers of policies don't bear the same accountability as the makers of actions—the practitioners—who have to implement the policies. The policymakers produce a policy for Iraq, Afghanistan, Somalia . . . or thirty-five years ago for Vietnam. The aims of their policies may be very fine and noble, and I have strongly supported our nation's aims in each of these cases . . . but not always the ways policies were implemented. When a policy fails, who takes the fall? The maker of the policy or the one who has tried to implement it—the general, or the ambassador on the ground, the implementer of policy, the practitioner? The one who takes the actions is always held accountable. Rarely do you see a policymaker held accountable for a failed policy. Rarely does he pay a price for a disaster he planned and mapped out.

Just as the command post must interact with the front line—*we've got to have both*—the foxhole view and the wonk view need each other. The ideal is to bring the theorist and the practitioner together, not to create competition between them. There has to be balance.

My concern right now is that the front-line view gets far less attention than it should.

I've seen a different world from the one theorists and policy folks are describing. It's a world that has gone through big changes during recent decades—changes the theorists and wonks have not given enough attention to. It's a world that is far more disordered and chaotic than the world most of us grew up in—the world of the Cold War. The chaotic new world screams out for a new kind of thinking and analysis that will reveal its true nature in all its dimensions and complexities. Our nation—and all first world nations—will need to take actions to prevent the chaos from spreading . . . or even from badly hurting us.

In the pages that follow, I'll offer the perspective of a fighter on the front lines of both war and peace. It's a view that has taken me at times to the trenches and at times into command posts. Whether in a trench or in a command post, I've always been on the front lines as a participant in the battle, not as an outside observer there for a look or a taste or for story material. The front-line perspective is not unique to me—I'm hardly alone in that experience—nor is it the only valid window into the reality of the battle, but it is a necessary window. You'll never get a true picture of the battle that does not include that front-line perspective.

I will try to describe the world that I see out there and the challenges it presents us, and to describe the actions we need to take to deal with it before it touches us in a way that threatens our well-being. Maybe even our survival.

CHAPTER THREE

BEYOND CHECKPOINT CHARLIE

Out of these troubled times . . . a new world order can emerge: freer from the threat of terror, stronger in the pursuit of justice, and more secure in the quest for peace. An era when the nations of the world, East and West, North and South, can prosper and live in harmony.
—George Herbert Walker Bush, 1990

How can a man in a cave out-communicate the world's leading communications society?
—Richard Holbrooke, 2001

The world changed in 1989. The change was seismic. Yet few out there even noticed the slightest tremors.

The change first hit me in Germany during a visit as a newly promoted brigadier general. As part of our orientation to senior-level rank, new one stars in our military go through what we call the Capstone Course—lectures, seminars, and visits to military facilities, with a special concentration on the areas where we are to be assigned (I was going to European Command—EUCOM). My Capstone group visited NATO and American bases and headquarters in Europe, including some in what was then West Berlin—an island deep behind the by-then crumbling Iron Curtain—an exciting, bustling, modern city, brimming over with life and energy. When we arrived in Berlin, the city had already become a major stage in the swiftly emerging drama, just as it had been a major stage in the Cold War drama.

Not long before we arrived, the Russians and East Germans had abandoned the Berlin wall. It was no longer a barrier. The guards had simply walked away. This strange new situation provided a fascinating opportunity for the bright and eager new one stars; and the hard-charging lieutenant from the U.S. Army's Berlin Brigade, who was stuck with our escort duties, seized on it. "Let's take a quick tour into East Berlin," he offered. "Why not?" we thought. Who was there to stop us? It was a great idea . . . *and* potentially a great adventure. It actually proved to be instructive; but we also encountered shocks and surprises. The first of these came when we crossed Checkpoint Charlie.

There it was, just as we'd seen it in innumerable spy movies, a major symbol of the Cold War, the gateway that more than any other spot on earth announced: "On our side freedom; on the other side totalitarian repression."

And then, poof, it was gone, unmanned overnight, without violence. They just left.

Passing by the now empty guard shacks and through the now un-manned gates was one of the strangest moments of my life. There we were, senior American military officers, driving through Checkpoint Charlie, and nobody noticed.

Beyond the checkpoint lay not just a different city; it was a different world. We had warped through time from modern, vibrant West Berlin back into the 1950s. East Berlin was a sad, drab, gray city. With the exception of a few movie-set façade avenues, we saw along the streets either old buildings, still pockmarked with World War II damage, or newer concrete and cinder block slabs, already shabby and dilapidated. Cars and trucks were few and grungy, belching smoke.

Many people were moving about on vintage 1950s bicycles—a stark contrast to the Mercedes and BMWs crowding the streets of West Berlin.

Later, we found a Soviet army casern, drove through the gate, got out of our van, and wandered around . . . another eerie moment. The Russian troops had no idea what to do about us. Were we bad guys? Were we conquerors? Were we friends? Paralyzed by this—and maybe by any—choice, they didn't do anything. They didn't know whether to shoot or salute. They just went about their business, like zombies. Some obviously had military duties. But you could see these duties no longer had purpose, and the Russians seemed to know it. On the streets and in the shops of the casern were the wives with their baby carriages and their children; like their husbands, they too looked like deer in headlights, their faces silently beseeching, "What's coming next for us? Where are we going to go?" These turned out to be very real and poignant questions. There was no place in Russia for them to go.

It hit me then that something had really changed; but I still could not see what that change was or be sure it wasn't all going to snap back.

After we drove back through the checkpoint, we stopped and knocked pieces off the wall—perhaps the chief symbol of the Cold War. It had now become a very different symbol.

I still have those shards from the Berlin wall.

Later in our European tour, we visited the U.S. Army European headquarters in Heidelberg, where we met with the chief of staff, a big, burly major general named Bill Burleson (nicknamed "The Bear").

Once again, here we were, a gaggle of one stars, all very experienced in military matters but in most cases much less knowledgeable in larger world issues. And here was this big, gruff general who, it turned out, had seen the big picture immediately and with brilliant clarity. When our group arrived in Europe, the full realization that the wall had come down and that the Soviet empire had ceased to exist had not *really* hit us. During a question period with Major General Burleson, we all trotted out our dutiful questions about our force presence in Europe, the Cold War, the Warsaw Pact, the status quo . . . all kinds of questions about the way it had been for the past fifty years. Our questions might have been appropriate a year, or even a few months, earlier.

As we asked our questions, Burleson just looked at us with the kind of bemused toleration we give to children. "No, no," he said, "it's *over*."

But we didn't really hear him. We still didn't get it, and we kept throwing at him our lineup of irrelevant questions. And all the while, he just kept looking at us and repeating, "It's over! IT'S OVER! . . . You guys don't get it. IT'S OVER! . . . Don't you guys understand? It's done. Finished. There's no more Cold War."

As we piled onto our small bus to move to the next place on our itinerary, his message slowly penetrated into me: "Something really big has changed. I don't quite understand it, but I have just seen physically in Berlin what this general is telling us. The old order no longer applies. It's gone. It's vanished. Something new is out there. The world has completely turned around overnight, but what does it mean?"

A memory from first grade suddenly popped into my head—carrying a pillowcase to school for our civil defense drills. When the siren sounded, we jumped under our desks, per instructions, and covered as much of ourselves as we could with our pillowcases; or else we filed down into the school basement that was the designated civil defense shelter with its yellow signs and its stacks of survival supplies. In those days citizens were building backyard underground bunkers and debating the morality of letting in, or not letting in, their less-prepared neighbors. For most of my life, over forty years, we had lived under those conditions—ready for Armageddon. Now it was over!

THE NEW WORLD DISORDER

We had witnessed a break in the total human environment as wide and deep as the seismic changes that followed World Wars I and II. In 1989, the Berlin Wall ceased to divide East and West. Meaning, the entire division between East and West—*the Iron Curtain itself*—had ceased to exist. The Soviet empire was then on the way down into the dustbin of history—unexpectedly departing the scene with an exhausted, impoverished whimper and not a world-shattering bang. The two great nuclear powers were pulling back from their fifty-year-long confrontation. The great nuclear war terror had faded. The Doomsday Clock was being reset. We could get rid of weapons of mass destruction. All over the world you could feel the—almost stunned—relief.

A fifty-year-long war—a "cold" war, yet a true war—had ended without leaving behind millions of dead, millions more maimed, millions more refugees, ruined and devastated cities, battle-scarred wastelands, disease, starvation . . . no Dresdens, no Hiroshimas, no Coventrys, no Stalingrads.

With the relaxing of international tensions came a conviction that a new world order of peace, prosperity, and security was approaching.

NATO? Who needs NATO? Defense spending? Hey, there's no need to throw all that money down the vast and insatiable military maw. Look what we can do with that money. Let's put it where we really need it. Tax cuts! A Peace Dividend! A new world order!

What would bring this wonderful new era to birth?

It was simply going to happen. It was obvious. It was natural. Everyone in the world would see the light. Or so it was believed.

It didn't happen.

Fifteen years later, who can deny that we are now engaged in a difficult, complex, and obviously long-term struggle to achieve the peace, stability, prosperity, and progressive growth we thought we had reached back then? In their place, we're seeing change upon change upon change, hitting us harder and harder with ever greater frequency. We haven't come to grips with the changes. We're seeing out there in the world ever more threatening disorder and chaos . . . and we seem confused and even helpless about how to face the threats, much less about how to take them on. We thought we were getting peace, and we got nothing like true peace. Our military has been far more engaged in all kinds of military actions after the Cold War than before it ended. We're not anywhere near where we thought we'd be now. Why not?

In the past century there have been three worldwide seismic changes, all producing major reorderings—after World War I, after World War II, and after the Cold War. By reordering, I mean a drastic change in the total environment—the balance of power among great states, the rules of interactions among states, and how the international economy functions. Such significant changes require a drastic change in thinking about, and approaches to, that new world. The effects generated by these reorderings unfold through many dimensions—in technology, in economics, in the means and techniques of production, in the use and availability of resources, in the conditions of labor, in the relations between nation-states, in their internal governance, and in the threats out there in the world.

As we all take all these conditions into account and form new approaches to the changed environment we will reformulate our national strategic thinking and restate our national purpose in a new kind of world.

At the end of World War I, Woodrow Wilson attempted to state a new purpose for the United States in the newly reordered world. In his view, America would use its newly gained power to influence the world for the better, and perhaps prevent the reemergence of the kinds of conditions that caused World War I. Wilson sought to export democracy and called for self-determination of peoples controlled by colonial empires—who also happened to be America's chief European allies.

For many reasons, the country and the Congress did not buy the president's new purpose. They weren't ready to abandon Washington's and Jefferson's counsel to focus on our own continental development and avoid "foreign entanglements."

Even in denying Wilson, the country stated a purpose—isolationism.

America has traditionally taken comfort in its secure borders and the broad oceans that both separate us from the dangers and entanglements of Europe and Asia and provide splendid highways for trade. Our drive was west, on our own continent and in our own hemisphere. In the early, growing years of our national existence, isolation had always been a blessed, easy choice for Americans. It was the wrong choice in the post–World War I world, as the next two decades proved.

The failure of many nations—not only ours—to build a new international order to replace the one ended by World War I brought on the unstable conditions that led to World War II.

After World War II, President Harry Truman and Secretary of State George Marshall reframed our nation's approach to another vastly changed world. That national purpose was the affirmation of freedom, through supporting independent countries, pushing for open economies, and deterring and containing the Soviet Union.

This time the new approach not only prevailed but evolved into the expanded national purpose that successfully carried us through the Cold War. Because the Truman approach worked so well, and was robust enough to withstand the stresses and pressures of several decades, we could easily take it as a natural development. Yet, at the time of its creation, the new strategic approach did not look so obvious; and it was much debated and resisted.

Truman and Marshall had seen the end of World War II, the first truly globe-spanning violent conflict; we had defeated fascism; our soldiers, sailors, and Marines had come home to a soon-booming economy—and a boom in babies. Life was wonderful. All was right

with the world! It would not have been hard to yield to the same isolationist temptation our nation succumbed to after World War I. But
they saw, as Wilson had, a need to influence the necessary change in
world conditions or be doomed to repeat the past.

In the immediate aftermath of the war, Truman and Marshall
launched their major initiatives. Their vision of international affairs
rested on these pillars: a stable and interlinked international economy, based on the Bretton Woods system, to avoid the economic disasters of the 1930s through ensuring greater coordination and cooperation; the Marshall Plan providing economic aid that was crucial to
the reconstruction of western Europe; strong international institutions—such as the United Nations, International Monetary Fund,
and World Bank—to provide forums for political and economic discussions; and containment of the Soviet Union by maintaining
American forces in Europe and creating an alliance committing
America to defend other countries—NATO.

Truman and his advisers also recognized that the American
government had to change in order to interact more effectively
with the new world that was being created. So they reformed the
military and created the National Security Council, the Joint
Chiefs, and the Central Intelligence Agency. They did all this with
optimism rather than in fear of a threat, for at that time few pre-
dicted that the Soviet Union would rise to become a challenging superpower. Sure, the Soviets were difficult, but not a threat; nothing
really to worry about.

Yet a handful of very wise men sensed that the world was reordering, though nobody could actually put a finger on what that might
mean or how it would play out over the next years and decades. These
men looked back at the post–World War I period, recognized the mis-
takes, and proposed new steps to influence the post–World War II reordering. Were these men wise and prescient enough to foresee the
Cold War, the need for a containment and deterrence strategy, or the
other big themes of the next fifty years? I very much doubt it.

They simply recognized that reordering doesn't necessarily bring a new and improved order—for that is not natural, especially if events are left to play out on their own (the 1920s and 1930s are a tragic witness to that truth). Leaving matters to take care of themselves is rolling the dice; anything might come up. The obvious alternative is to put the odds in your favor by exercising some influence over events while understanding that fully controlling them is impossible.

By the late 1940s and early 1950s, when the Soviet Union emerged as a superpower and tested nuclear weapons and long-range rockets, the Truman and Marshall reforms had already proved themselves. We were well positioned to deal with the rising threat and to control most events.

Meanwhile, the two superpowers were busily learning from history, examining and analyzing the lessons learned from the run-ups to the two world wars.

In August 1914, nobody really thought Europe was going to war. Some mad anarchist assassinated an archduke. Nobody really worried. People were on vacation. La Belle Époque remained blissfully belle. Even when somebody set the war plans in motion by pressing the buttons that called up the reserves and got the trains moving (the plans were on automatic), everybody kept calm. After all, cooler, wiser, more diplomatically astute heads would sort out the mess. That fantasy ended with the thunder of the guns.

In 1938 and 1939, the cool, wise diplomats were blind to the Nazis' lust to consume Europe, even though the Nazis' intentions were obvious.

In the 1950s and 1960s, the two superpowers had strong motives to avoid those pre–World War I and pre–World War II pitfalls. They were armed with weapons that could destroy the world. This was the era of "fail safe" and "mutually assured destruction." Both the USSR and the United States recognized how easy it would be to get lost in a rapidly moving sequence of events that nobody could stop. They understood how small events in out-of-the-way places could domino into a nuclear exchange. They carefully watched over and managed these little events. Even when they battled each other in surrogate fights or committed to support countries like Vietnam, they held back. Their support was always conditional. Why didn't the United States invade North Vietnam? Because an invasion would have forced the Russians and the Chinese to openly join the fight. From there to nuclear doom was not a great leap.

Everyone saw the chain.

The year 1962 brought the Cuban Missile Crisis, when both sides climbed higher up the chain than ever before. Did the Soviets imagine that putting a few missiles and a brigade of Russians into Cuba would bring the world to the brink of nuclear exchange? I doubt it. This was simply another move in the zero-sum game, where everything counts. They now "owned" Cuba and Castro; they made a move in the game—Knight to QB3. The next thing we knew we were perilously close to the "Big One."

But both powers stopped their dangerous ascent toward madness before they came to the end of the chain. Every analysis of the Cuban Missile Crisis shows that both sides feared they would lose control.

It was the most dangerous time in the history of man. We could have literally destroyed all human life on the planet. Yet, it was simple and understandable. All sides knew the dangers of miscalculations and were clear on the rules of the game.

That reality became patently clear to me one cold day in the 1980s on a visit to an ICBM missile silo in the Midwest. As a young air force missile technician and I squeezed down the side of the massive missile on a narrow scaffold, I thought about how the awesome destructive power I was straddling could be unleashed if a miscalculation or irrational act could not be prevented. Though each superpower had a competitive strategy, there was control, and as a result, a strange kind of stability.

The end of the Cold War changed all that. The lid came off. The manageable, superpower-imposed stability fell away, and nothing took its place. We expected a new world order of peace and prosperity to bless the Earth. We could not have been more wrong. Instead of global peace and prosperity, all the snakes came out, with consequences that are still unfolding. The superpowers, now reduced to one, were no longer there to buy off problems, as in the previous zero-sum game, in order to add even the most inconsequential nation to their spheres of influence. The new world order turned out to be a new world disorder. The so-called peace dividend went the way of the Berlin wall and Checkpoint Charlie.

We had passed through a seismic shift on a par with the end of World Wars I and II, but we didn't treat it as such; we didn't make the big moves that the events warranted and didn't come up with a new strategic approach to influence the shape of a post–Cold War environment, maybe because there was no big, violent, climactic finish to the Cold War era. There was a critical need to restate our purpose in strategic terms: our strategic purpose guides policy, guides the transformation of the military, guides economic direction, guides diplomacy, guides our social influences and our cultural interactions, and determines alliances. It is the foundation for all the actions we take in the world to ensure stability, security, and peace.

But because the shift came at the end of a cold war—a radically different kind of war—we didn't see the same level of effect in "vanquished" nations. (We couldn't really even call them vanquished.) At the ends of major wars, you have collapsed societies and you have radically changing environments. These happened at the end of the Cold War, yet in the West, people had a naïve belief that once we'd lifted a repressive system off the backs of people behind the Iron Curtain, the Iron Curtain nations were going to automatically flower into secure and prosperous democracies.

In some nations, as in Poland, where the Soviet system had replaced viable pre-Soviet institutions, the withering away of the Soviet system opened a path for the renewal of their pre-Soviet institutions. These nations quickly returned to democracy and Western-style economies. But elsewhere in the former empire, democracy has been much more hit or miss.

In 1989, we found ourselves in a unipolar world. The United States was the *one* superpower, with such vast power that no competitor could directly threaten its existence. After earlier wars, a handful of dominant powers—and maybe a few more regional powers—had been left standing. This time only one really tall man was left standing.

For the first time in history, a major conflict had ended without overwhelming violence. The end of the Soviet empire came with a sudden—and *shocking*—collapse; it did not take many decades, like Rome's decline.

Yet, no one foresaw that the new emerging environment would be so hostile. Certainly no one believed that a complex witches' brew of events and conditions would converge in what had been the marginal part of the world—that part outside the core zones of the two superpowers—that would affect the whole world. Up until then, stable, or first world, nations could choose to ignore problems in the third world. Those destabilizing problems could be kept away from our borders.

Our expectation of peace, security, and prosperity was so powerful that we blinded ourselves to what was actually going on in the world, to how it could affect us, and to what we had to do about it.

At European Command, I was assigned to the Operations Directorate (J–3) at our Stuttgart headquarters, as the deputy director. When there was a heightened action mode in an operations shop, I also headed up the Crisis Action Team—or CAT—to deal with crises and other fast-moving and difficult events. During my two years at EUCOM, either the CAT or a full-fledged Battle Staff (a larger crisis management staff) was up and running all the time. New world order or no, a lot of garbage was hitting the fan with increasing frequency.

The 1990 Gulf War was the first major crisis to hit. Everyone knew this crisis was going to be managed by a new set of rules, which were going to be written by the one remaining superpower. The world watched carefully to see how the rules would turn out.

Would they reflect an enlightened, forward-looking, and multinational approach to a very different kind of crisis than those we had faced in the Cold War? Or would they perhaps reflect a more backward-looking or even isolationist view of the world?

To their great credit, the first Bush administration looked forward. The new rules emphasized international cooperation, the United Nations, and coalitions to deal with Saddam Hussein, who had invaded Kuwait and threatened Saudi Arabia, and they were well received. They showed promise of a new cooperation and collective direction in dealing with destabilizing crises . . . a promise that was not completely realized.

This first Gulf War was followed by our intervention in northern Iraq to save the Kurds. During my EUCOM tour we also had to deal with all kinds of small but difficult crises in Africa: Liberia had gone to hell, and we had to conduct noncombatant evacuations in Zaire and Sierra Leone. Lebanon was still a mess. Our intel guys looking at the Balkans didn't like what they were seeing: "Yugoslavia is like a cheap suitcase," they were saying. "It's going to come apart in a heartbeat." They were right.

Meanwhile, who among us was really aware that the USSR was made up of "separate" republics defined by ethnic identity? But now that the empire was breaking up, we had to look at all kinds of new nations fissioned off from the old union, all with deeply uncertain futures. Ukraine? Belarus? Uzbekistan? Who were they? Where were they going? Now that they were independent nations, they had to work out their own identities. Eastern Europe, having escaped Soviet domination, looked west.

The old order was coming apart in myriad ways. And in the cockpit of EUCOM's Operations Directorate, I was at the heart of our responses to the disintegration. From there I could clearly see a downward spiraling trend that was being mirrored in the areas of responsibility of the other regional commands.

SHAPING A NEW ORDER

Not every American leader was blind to the rapidly emerging international realities. Some recognized that letting events take their "natural" course was staking too much on rolling the dice. Serious and thoughtful efforts were made to shape and influence significant, potentially destabilizing conditions in the former empire.

General Jack Galvin (United States), the EUCOM commander, was a soldier-statesman in the manner of George Marshall, and one of the most intelligent and thoughtful men I've had the honor of knowing. His great vision, strategic depth, insightfulness, statesmanship, and military competence proved priceless assets as we tried to face up to the changed world brought on by the collapse of the Soviets.

Galvin's sense that we had to take a stronger hand in the reordering of the former Soviet Union and the other nations of Eastern Europe inspired him to reach out to their obviously confused and disoriented military leadership with an offer of help, friendship, and encouragement—and with an underlying aim to dissuade them from interfering with efforts to transform the communist dictatorships into democracies.

Galvin sent American senior officers (I was one of them) to Moscow and Warsaw Pact nations to meet with their East European counterparts to discuss issues of mutual concern, and more broadly to serve as models for positive change. The meetings were productive, given our new friends' traumatized state. The former Soviet bloc military—for the most part—stayed out of politics.

During this same time, Galvin was putting out fires in his own house. Advocates of the peace dividend back in Washington were questioning the need for NATO. "The big threat's gone," they were saying. "Why do we need a military presence in Europe? Let's bring back our military to our own shores, significantly cut back their numbers, save big on military costs, and free up our resources for other pressing needs."

On the face of it, this was a reasonable position. In fact, it failed to recognize that NATO itself had metamorphosed into a different—and much more important and effective—kind of organization than the one that for fifty years had blocked Soviet expansion west. It had become not just an alliance set up to defend the participating countries, but, as I wrote in my earlier book, *Battle Ready,* "an organization where competent, responsible nations working closely together could actually get important things done that they could not accomplish on their own. In so doing, they were showing the rest of the world how to do it. NATO had become an irreplaceable model for everyone else."

Galvin counseled caution and careful consideration before anyone made big changes in NATO that we might regret later. He and others understood the value of NATO as an institution for cooperation and order. He and others knew that drawing down in NATO would create concerns about American dependability among our European allies. And he and others knew that it is far easier to destroy an institution than to build one.

Though he knew that some force reductions were inevitable and that NATO might have to be reorganized, he relentlessly asked Washington, "How many troops do we need? How many can we safely cut? How should we be organized for the new world order? What new missions could we expect to take on?" And: "What is the purpose of NATO? What do we need it for? What must we do to support that?" In spite of his efforts, numbers in Europe were brought down quickly, sometimes precipitously quickly, and morale plummeted. Yet he still kept pressing for caution and reason.

Galvin knew NATO had to be reshaped to deal with the new conditions, and he clearly saw what that shape had to be—what NATO eventually became: it later grew to include several former Warsaw Pact nations, and its mission later changed to include operations outside of its normal European area.

He realized, finally, that even though the end of the Cold War had not left behind widespread physical devastation, the "losers" in the war still required the assistance of a program like the Marshall Plan, which had brought renewed life to a dying Europe fifty years earlier.

There were powerful humanitarian reasons to back such an effort: the peoples of the former Soviet bloc absolutely needed aid if they were going to get back on their feet. But there were equally powerful security reasons as well: by rebuilding institutions ruined by communist incompetence and misrule—or in some cases building new institutions from scratch—we would be promoting stability and preventing the reemergence of conditions that might later threaten us. Never forget the aftermath of World War I when western nations failed to address and shape the unstable conditions that led directly to World War II.

That torch was taken up by Secretary of State James Baker and Ambassador Richard Armitage. By the end of 1991, it was clear to Baker that the new world order was a delusion; and he recognized that *something* had to be done to bring about a genuine new order in the former Soviet Union. His vision for achieving this was to launch the new Marshall Plan that was Galvin's dream. Baker also realized that this vision—a truly gigantic undertaking called Operation Provide Hope—could never be accomplished unilaterally, even by the United States. We would need the support and resources of other developed nations. Many other questions obviously had to be answered, and many uncertainties clarified, before this monster project could bear fruit.

The plan was to start simply, with the hope that others would hitch onto the wagon as it rolled forward. Baker dispatched Armitage to Europe to direct the efforts. And General Galvin dispatched me to Armitage to handle EUCOM's support for them. Armitage—a Naval Academy graduate, a one-time Navy Seal, and a Vietnam combat vet—brought to the job a long career in government in both the Defense and State Departments, where he'd been an ambassador at large (that is, a troubleshooter). Though Armitage was initially skeptical of my presence on his team and suspicious of EUCOM's motives in sending me, I quickly demonstrated good faith by setting up the machinery needed for the operation and got it moving quickly and efficiently.

Initially it was to be a humanitarian airlift of food, medicines, and other supplies to the former Soviet republics. Most of these supplies came out of prepositioned stocks that we had long ago stashed in secure locations throughout western Europe to be used in the event of the hot war that never happened.

As time passed, and as it became clear to Armitage that he and I shared troubleshooting experience, we became friends.

Provide Hope was officially launched in January 1992. From that day until the operation ended, Armitage and I flew all over Europe and the former USSR—dealing with NATO and the European Union, dealing with the Russian leadership, dealing with local officials, coordinating, assessing success and failure.

The humanitarian airlift lasted about a month, during which we delivered 2,100 tons of needed supplies to twenty-one different locations in the various republics. I remained assigned to Provide Hope for the next three months, getting increasingly involved for Armitage in economic- and political-related activities on behalf of the operation. Meanwhile, Armitage worked ceaselessly to bring about the goals Secretary Baker had set for the project . . . even as it became more and more evident that the vision was not going to be realized. The other developed nations were simply not interested in coming to the party. The absence of obvious physical devastation after the Cold War, the euphoria brought on by the sudden arrival of peace, and the understandable desire to use their newly freed up resources for their own people, meant that other nations were uninterested in an American-inspired multilateral program to help former enemies. The need was not apparent. It was not a time of all for one, one for all. It was a time when weary nations wanted to look inward in establishing their priorities. Soon afterwards, the Germans had to pay for their own reunification. Fifteen years later, they still have not completely recovered from that hit.

The failure of Provide Hope to excite other nations and international organizations (such as the UN and the EU) still remains a badly missed opportunity. If it had been successfully launched, the turmoil and instabilities that later badly hurt Russia, its separated republics, Yugoslavia, and other countries might have been avoided.

THE PERFECT STORM

The collapse of the Soviet Union and the subsequent end of the Cold War created an opening for the formulation of a new order, a new set of rules, and a new world environment. It set the conditions for swarms of new forces—centered on what is now called globalization, but going way beyond that—to accelerate and rush into the vacuum that followed the collapse of one side of the bipolar power structure and the lack of interest by the remaining side to influence events in any major way. Some of these new forces may yet prove to be beneficial; others are already proving dangerous and disruptive. All of them have been whirling around unchecked. They've gathered, gained strength, shot out in all kinds of unexpected directions. They have become a Perfect Storm.

Globalization

Globalization—the worldwide integration of economies and societies—has grown almost faster than we can measure, exploding into every interaction that peoples of the world conduct.

Some love it. Some don't.

To its supporters it promises worldwide economic development and trade; ever greater technological progress; ever greater productivity; ever greater ease of transit and mobility; ever greater rationalization of global production and services; and greater ability to establish global systems that ensure fairness, balance, shared prosperity, equal justice, and responsible stewardship of the earth's resources.

To its detractors it threatens increased economic inequality; environmental degradation; exploitation of the third world; uncontrolled depletion of resources; loss of cultural and national identity; and the rise of uncontrolled non-state entities.

Who's right? Who knows?

I can't possibly say. Only the future will tell.

We can't be sure where globalization is leading us; but we can clearly see its effects. We can see worldwide information networks and globe-spanning corporations; courts with worldwide jurisdiction; collective monetary systems; global transfers of jobs and production; global migrations and diasporas; global competition for ever-decreasing resources; and growing numbers of borderless organizations.

Should we be concerned? Do these issues threaten our national security? Do they threaten loss of our national identity and control of our national destiny? These are troubling questions for a superpower and for other first world nations. Wise leaders must step up to the plate and answer them.

Such questions are even more troubling for the third world. Third world nations are clearly on the whip end of the new world ordering . . . or disordering.

Globalization is not a single, simple force that plays out everywhere the same way. It is a confluence of forces (many predating the fall of the Soviet empire) that hits different nations, peoples, and cultures in different ways and at different tempos—that is, at different rates of change. Nearly everyone in the world has been affected by globalization, but for some peoples and cultures the changes have washed over them faster than they can adapt to them.

And even those elements and trends that seem benign have troubling aspects.

Take for example globe-spanning corporations—an important indicator of the rise of globalization. They improve efficiency. They improve productivity. They move factories and outsource jobs to those parts of the world where production is cheapest. Technological innovations are quickly spread throughout the world—a good thing. Components of products are manufactured here, there, anywhere; assembled somewhere else; and then marketed perhaps somewhere else. And all this means that consumers pay less. This is desirable.

But to whom are these new kinds of corporations responsible?

The collapse of the old world order freed corporations from many kinds of state control, including their identities as business organizations headquartered in a specific country. Even if they might have a company "headquarters" in New York City, London, Tokyo, or Seoul, do these new global businesses think of themselves as American companies? British companies? Japanese companies? Korean? What restraints can individual nations place on them when their corporate identities are spread everywhere?

Is this good or bad?

If trade, productivity, ever increasing stock values, and other economic benefits are our exclusive goals, then globe-spanning corporations are unquestionably good. But can we be certain of the consequences that follow from an international corporation's ability to avoid external, national controls? Nations with a solid rule of law and strong consumer protections will probably not suffer seriously nasty consequences from global corporations. But what are the effects of their operations in nations when such institutions are weak? Should we concede authority to international organizations to place restraints and controls on them?

We in the industrialized world have only tangentially had to come to grips with questions like these. And globalization poses many such questions. We still don't understand totally how globalization will affect us and everyone else. We know it's changing the old world order. We know it's changing the economic balance of the world. But we haven't fully grasped how to manage it, how to protect ourselves from its bad side, or how to encourage and promote its good side.

The result—yet more confusion as we struggle to make sense of the new world disorder.

The Weakening of Sovereignty

Under the old rules and conventions, the only interactions between peoples were through the nation-state. Issues of sovereignty were all dominant; and nationalism was the strongest, most driving ideology in modern history. The UN was founded to manage nationalism. It was created to lessen frictions between nation-states, but also to *protect* the sovereignty of those same nation-states and to subordinate itself to that sovereignty.

Nationalism and national sovereignty no longer carry either the force or the physical and cultural integrity they once did.

Sovereign nations are no longer autonomous and all powerful . . . no longer—as it was once thought—billiard balls knocking against other billiard balls; but more like human beings themselves: living, moving, breathing only within their environment. Nations can't exist isolated from the global environment. And neither can they isolate themselves from the forces that are becoming increasingly dominant in the global environment.

Suddenly we're in a world where national autonomy and an isolated form of national integrity may not always matter.

Since the end of the Cold War, the UN, NATO, and others have conducted many peacekeeping and other interventions in "sovereign" nations—in the Balkans, in Iraq, in Rwanda, in Congo, in Somalia, in East Timor (Indonesia). Because of respect for national sovereignty, such interventions were virtually unthinkable during the Cold War. Such interventions have become commonplace because sovereignty is no longer the potent force it once was.

In earlier times, sovereignty defined how to determine victory or defeat in war. Now such determinations are much more muddled.

In the twentieth century, we could defeat the military forces of a sovereign nation-state and expect to dictate terms. That defined victory. But not today. Unlike Japan and Germany, which accepted defeat and capitulation and moved on, the people of a defeated nation do not today accept or recognize capitulation or move on. The old rules and conventions no longer apply. The sovereign nation-states—ours and theirs—no longer settle the question of when and how the war ends. Victory is not defined by the victorious nation-state dictating terms to a defeated one. Other dimensions come into play.

In addition to global corporations, other non-state entities have emerged and proliferated. Many have become major power sources with international influence. These organizations come in many forms and shapes—some evil, some good, some somewhere in between. Their numbers are on the rise, and they have increasing influence.

International terrorist and violent extremist networks have a global reach; and organized crime is now also global. The Cali Cartel, the Russian mafia, and other criminal networks have resources, assets, and reach that exceed most nation-states. Al Qaeda succeeded in inflicting more damage on America's homeland than our enemies did in World War II. Warlords carve out fiefdoms and dictate to weakened governments or fill the vacuum created by collapsed states in many parts of the world.

International, regional, and subregional political entities like the EU, ASEAN (Association of South-East Asian Nations), and the African Union have varying degrees of influence. The EU—distinct from its component states—is a major world player.

Non-governmental organizations (NGOs) are proliferating— and not just the ones handing out food and medicine. Some work with nations to mediate violent conflicts and to build or rebuild vital national institutions in such fields as education, health care, justice, and security. The International Court of Justice decides international legal cases. These and similar organizations exceed the ability of most nation-states in resources, influence, and control.

Religion-based organizations have grown, and powerful religious ideologies have replaced political ideologies as the foundation of many movements around the world. Stalin dismissed the power of the pope: "How many divisions does he have?" But I wonder if Stalin would take back that remark in light of the role Pope John Paul II played in the downfall of the Soviet Union.

Porous Borders

Nation-states will not soon wither away. But their ability to solely control or influence events within and outside their borders has declined. States no longer control vital aspects of peoples' lives; the nation-state identity as the primary source of community interaction is weakening. In the past, nation-states controlled or filtered information. They were the central source for communication links, networks, and media. The people did not have direct access to one another except on a one-on-one personal basis. Now all that's ending. The information flow through internet and satellite links can't be totally controlled.

Borders mean far less than they once did. The walls that once kept peoples and nations safely apart now show gaping holes. Geographical barriers—oceans, deserts, mountain ranges—no longer stop migrants seeking new homes. Diseases like AIDS, West Nile virus, and ever more deadly forms of flu; criminals and terrorists; every kind of idea, doctrine, and extremist ideology; weapons of mass destruction; computer viruses . . . all can easily and quickly move from country to country. Disorder and chaos in places we don't want to think about leap across oceans and bite people and places we very much care about.

When I have a computer problem, I talk to some technical support expert in India who speaks perfect American English and calls himself Sammy, not Sanjay. My computer is flooded with spam scams from Nigeria. Circumventing government controls is getting easier and easier. If my government wants to prevent me from reading some publication or seeing some movie, I download them from a satellite link.

We live in a world where outsiders are getting increasingly involved in other peoples' problems . . . because their problems are increasingly involving outsiders. Problems are not just *your* problems; they're *our* problems.

I go to some tropical country: "Quit cutting down your rainforest," I demand.

"What business is it of yours?" they ask. "It's our rainforest.

"Because when you cut down your rainforest, you change the climate where I live."

Or I say, "Quit abusing your people."

"What business is it of yours?"

"It's my business when your people start washing up on my shores."

Or people in some country start blaming me for their problems because of my support for their repressive government. And some of the more extreme elements in the country may bomb resorts where Americans vacation.

We may certainly want to keep this government as an ally, because it's in our interest. But we may also want to go to that government and ask, "Hey, friend, help us out. Democratize. Pay more attention to human rights and democratic processes. It's best for you. And it's best for us."

The question then becomes, How do we make ourselves safe in this newly emerging world? Can we do it by stopping all the threats and problems at our own borders? Or will we follow a wiser course by addressing the instabilities and threats out there where they are born?

Americans will naturally gravitate toward isolation. They will always hope to erect impassable barriers. "We can make ourselves secure from the instability," we like to tell ourselves. "How can we defend our borders?"

Americans want a Star Wars missile defense and homeland security. We want to check every shipping container in every port. We want to block off visas to keep out potentially dangerous visitors or immigrants. "Okay, if the world's problems are washing up on my shores, then we must take the measures necessary to ensure that no longer happens."

In the long run, that is not going to work. If our chief line of defense is our own borders, then the bad guys are going to get through to us. A city-killing nuclear, biological, or chemical weapon will now fit in a backpack that can be transported into a country any number of ways. Many weapons don't require transport across borders. Enemies can beam directions for making them from anywhere in the world. They can even hurt us seriously without violent means. They can get into our information systems and destroy our databases. They can cause chaos in any number of vital systems—banking, air traffic control, electricity.

We aren't going to prevent diseases from spreading over our borders. Once it has started there, we aren't going to prevent environmental destruction from spreading here. We can't build iron bubbles around ourselves.

Though the defensive course is attractive, it can't work.

Changing Identities

Who am I?

The question can be asked by an Iraqi Kurd; a member of the Muslim community in Europe; a Latino migrant worker in the United States; or an Indian employee in a hotel in the Middle East.

For them and many millions of others out there, their answers to the question will be far from obvious. Their search for identity—or their assertion of identity—will be answered in far different terms from those laid out in the old rules.

At one time—especially in Europe—a nation-state was defined as the geographical domain of a specific ethnic group or tribe—Italians, Germans, French, Poles, Hungarians. In the old order, wars between European nations were wars between tribes—Germans versus French, Greeks versus Turks. But in many parts of the world, and even in Europe, ethnic identities may now no longer relate to geographical boundaries, and peoples may no longer take their identities from the nation-states where they reside. The societal diasporas have exploded, and assimilation has become more difficult.

National identities have declined in favor of other forms of identity. This is especially true in the case of the states created artificially as a result of colonialism. Before the British created Iraq, there was no "Iraqi" nation or "Iraqi" people. There was no previously existing "Iraqi" identity. The same situation exists in many African nations. How many Nigerians consider themselves to be Nigerians first and Ibo or Yoruba second? These artificially created states have been frail and unstable from their births.

People are not necessarily losing their old forms of identity, but the forms of identity are changing, the makeup of societies is changing, and the emphases people put on their own identity—the ways people look at themselves—are changing: "What's more important to me? My country? My ethnicity or race? My religion?"

What does it mean to be French? Millions of North African Muslims are now French. But they are hardly French in the same sense that Jacques Chirac is French or that Juliette Binoche is French.

What does it mean to be American? Millions of Hispanic peoples from Latin America—ethnically Native Americans—have now become American citizens, and are now in the majority throughout much of our West and Southwest—or will be soon. The Indians are taking back the country.

When Marshal Tito ran Yugoslavia, he kept the lid on the entire country; and people might actually have considered themselves Yugoslavs . . . though they also thought of themselves as Serbs, Albanians, Bosnians, or Muslims, Orthodox Christians, or Catholics. But after he died, the old order collapsed, the lid popped, and nobody thought of himself as Yugoslav. All of a sudden, this person is a Serb. That person is an Albanian. That one is a Bosnian. That one is a Muslim. A Croat. Eastern Orthodox. Catholic. Suddenly, identity issues became central to the political dynamic . . . religious identities, ethnic identities, tribal identities.

Something similar has happened in Iraq. Under Saddam, everyone in Iraq was Iraqi, they had no choice . . . though they were also Sunni, Shiite, Chaldean, Kurd, Turcoman, Assyrian, or Christian. Now that we have knocked out Saddam's regime, can we count on everyone in Iraq still holding on to an Iraqi identity?

We invaded Iraq believing that Iraqis would all keep thinking of themselves as Iraqis. We went in to free all Iraqis *as* Iraqis. But it turns out they didn't think of themselves as Iraqis. They wanted to be free as Shiites or Kurds. And it turns out that the minority Sunnis were reluctant to give up the privileges, powers, and ascendancy they had long held over all the other Iraqis.

In Central Asia, after the Uzbeks, Kazakhs, Turcomans, Kirghiz, and Tajiks threw off the Soviet yoke, their first priority was to return to their own languages and traditions. Yet few of the Central Asians had a clear idea about what exactly were their national identities.

When I visited Uzbekistan, the Uzbeks were searching their history for evidence of their Uzbek identity, building museums to celebrate their glorious past, and claiming Tamurlane as their patriarch. But Tamurlane was not an Uzbek leader; he was a Mongol leader, the product of an invading and conquering people who subjugated the Uzbeks.

Do Muslims think of themselves primarily by their national, ethnic, or religious identity? Some go one way; some go other ways.

Why does a young Saudi decide to go blow himself up in Kashmir for an issue between Pakistanis and Indians? Why does another young Saudi go to fight in Afghanistan against the Soviets? Or go to fight in Iraq against Americans? They feel a religious identity affinity that is stronger than their national identity.

In America we tend to identify by ethnic origin—Italian, Hispanic, Native American, African American, Pakistani, WASP. In Europe, communities are more often identified by religious affiliation. In Europe, they talk about the Muslim Community, not about the Pakistani Brit or the French Algerian or the French Moroccan.

A professor friend of mine in Britain—a British citizen whose ethnic roots are Pakistani and whose religion is Islam—feels Europeans are reinforcing the Muslim identities of immigrant communities who come from all over the map. Europeans are dumping this enormous, multinational hodgepodge into a single crucible—Muslim. What besides their religion do Irish Catholics, Italian Catholics, German Catholics, Hispanic Catholics, and Filipino Catholics have in common? Would an imposed religious identity in the United States have made assimilation more difficult for them? Does an encouraged or imposed religious identity foster greater problems in today's charged environment? When Europeans—intentionally or unintentionally—make the mosque the central point of focus for everyone who happens to be Muslim, do they create conditions that give radical imams far greater influence than they would otherwise have?

Mass Migrations

The decline of the nation-state and the breakdown of secure national borders have taken the lid off the normal constraints on legal and illegal migrations. To paraphrase the Southwest Airlines ad, "You are now free to move about the world." Millions of people all over the world are moving out of their home countries—either because the grass is greener somewhere else, or more likely because life is unbearable at home.

Normally, people want to live where they have their families and their roots. And normally, it takes a strongly motivated person to rip out his roots and abandon his old life and family. In the eighteenth, nineteenth, and early twentieth centuries, as the American national myth has it, the motivation for immigration was dreams and daring.

Today people are more likely to risk the move because the chaos, instability, or violence back home have made their lives intolerable.

But the risks of moving are great.

Many die attempting to cross the Sonora desert from Mexico to the United States. Many die attempting to cross the sea from Haiti or Cuba to the United States, or from North Africa to Italy, or from Asia to Australia.

Once they make it to America or Europe, the migrants—both legal and illegal—often transfer to the first world the instabilities and chaos endemic in the third world; and so they put strains on a nation's security and social systems that its systems may not be able to handle. There are humanitarian issues, religious tolerance issues, political issues (they can eventually vote, and they need services, which cost money). Extreme Islamist immigrants bring in mosques and leaders who encourage radicalism and violence.

In the past, immigrants into the United States normally migrated into already-existing immigrant communities. We created enclaves—Italian communities, Irish communities, Jewish communities, German communities—which were eventually stepping stones to assimilation.

Today in cities like New York or Los Angeles, there are Russian communities, Chinese communities, and Arab communities. Will these, as before, prove to be stepping stones to assimilation in a generation or two? It's hard to say—yet, you can now see encouraging signs in places such as New York, like modest, young veiled Muslim women wearing slacks and T-shirts that read, "YOGA AND PILATES."

This country has a tradition of assimilation; Europe does not. In the past, when you thought of Western or of Northern Europe, you thought of white men. Exclusively white societies are everywhere a thing of the past. But what will then be the impact on these societies of a more varied society that doesn't have a central, dominant tribe, or the tribal recognition or identity they once had? Migrations to Europe from former colonies have generated frictions that Europeans aren't handling well. European birth rates are declining. European economies need the workers, but their societies have a hard time handling the cultural and religious differences the workers bring with them.

On the other hand, if conditions are made more tolerable back in their home countries, people will stay home. In the previous century, many of the best, brightest, and most highly educated emigrated from India. But as capacity was built up and good jobs became increasingly available, the best and the brightest decided to stay home. Though outsourcing to India became a problem for the American economy and employment picture, India is far more stable, peaceful, and prosperous than it was a few years ago.

Anyone who fails to understand what these changes mean, and what they bring to countries and societies, will be lost in today's world. Anyone who tries to apply mid-twentieth-century templates to these problems will find himself lost, confused, and powerless to handle them.

Failed States

Collapsing states and states on the edge are *always* bad news.

They breed wars, secessions, and regional chaos. They can become sanctuaries for criminals of all sorts, predators, warlords, hostile non-state entities, extremist movements, and far-reaching terrorist networks. They can be sources of massive illegal migrations;

generate global environmental or health problems; unleash religious radicalism and horrible ethnic or religious hatreds that spread beyond their local borders; and produce humanitarian disasters on a massive scale.

A given state's incapability may be in a few areas or it may be in general. And these instabilities may cause it to collapse, or they may not. Some states simply live with their instabilities and struggle along. These states may never collapse and fail, but they are weak.

The ability of fragile states to survive in the current environment has become more problematic. Some states that were artificial creations from colonial eras are coming apart. Others that have not had viable natural resources or an advantageous geography find survival difficult. Still others with significant internal problems and strife lack the capacities necessary to prevail over the forces destroying them. These increasingly become global problems that can't be ignored.

All the changes put in motion in 1989 have at best generated mixed results on this front. The promises of better economic, political, social, and humanitarian conditions have been realized by a few societies. A great number of societies have experienced the opposite, facing such disturbing negative conditions as an increase in economic polarity (the rich get richer and the poor get poorer); degradation of the environment and resulting destructive climatic effects; overpopulation of regions unable to sustain demographic growth; and the devastating effects of exploding urbanization in the third world. Multi-million-inhabitant third world cities rarely have a viable physical infrastructure, or political and social structure, and they breed every kind of social, health, and environmental evil.

⚡

Even seemingly good things can generate negative effects. The information age has given us unprecedented access to information and the ability to rapidly move it all over the globe. That information, however, does not come with an inherent measure of accuracy and truth, or with any way to control or counter its undesirable messages. It can be moved by vast global networks to distort, incite, propagandize, or corrupt. It can be used by non-state entities such as Al Qaeda to direct, control, and inspire followers.

The easy access to ever more sophisticated technology makes our lives better, yet it also allows terrorist groups to connect and command their networks through cheap throwaway cell phones, faxes, and Internet sites. It gives them easy access to destructive components and the knowledge of how to use them to cause the greatest harm.

The end result of the confluence of the collapse of the East and the confusion of the West with the unleashed new forces of globalization has been a growing environment of instability. We have not thought through the implications of this new chaotic world and how it affects our security. Nor have we thought through how to deal with it.

We consistently throw at it our one power punch—the military—even as the very nature of war itself is passing through a perfect storm brought on by the new world disorder. The new warfare requires a new kind of warrior and a new kind of military.

CHAPTER FOUR

THE NEW FACE OF WAR

The army we're fighting is different from the army we gamed against.
—Lieutenant General William Wallace
Commander, U.S. Army V Corps, Iraq, 2003

As the world changed, the front lines—the battlefields, the scenes of military action—changed with it, though predictably many leaders in the military didn't immediately notice the changes.

In the first thirty-three years of its existence, from 1945 to 1978, the United Nations conducted only thirteen peacekeeping or observer operations aimed at defusing crises and building stability. Over the next decade, 1978 to 1988, the UN launched no new operations of these kinds; but since then, the numbers have exploded, with forty-seven conducted from 1988 to the present.

A similar increase has occurred in international humanitarian missions during this period. Because many of these operations faced a mix of humanitarian and security problems, they became known as "complex emergency operations."

In spite of this explosion of peacekeeping and humanitarian actions, failed or incapable states with massive problems were still allowed to degrade into crisis—the point of no return—while reluctant, capable nations dallied over intervention. This was further evidence of the seismic change created by the collapse of the dual superpower structure.

When crises had spun out of control, our nation now and again chose to thrust ill-thought-out interventions upon our military—at a time when our military was especially unprepared for them. In those early days of the "new world disorder," our military was trying to reinvent itself in response to rapid reductions in forces and budgets. The military leadership did not expect or welcome a sudden plunge into nontraditional missions.

In taking on the new challenge, they decided to follow the path of least effort. The easiest solution was to play down these new missions—initially called Military Operations Other Than War (MOOTW—pronounced "mootwa"). "Mootwa missions aren't *real* war," they told themselves. "So we don't have to give them *real* attention." Or as one very senior general put it, "Real men don't do mootwa." To the military, the business of war was about major conventional combat operations, and that is where they wanted to stay focused. They looked at these new missions as a temporary nuisance, not worthy of more than minor adjustments in doctrine, training, education, and organization.

But "mootwa" they did, in Somalia, Bosnia, Haiti, Bangladesh, East Timor, Rwanda, and many other places. Like them or not, these new kinds of operations have become a central focus of our military efforts. They demand officers and troops with very different kinds of training, outlooks, and capabilities. The battlefield is different; the front lines are different; the foxhole is different.

THE NEW BATTLEFIELD

My first plunge into these strange new missions came in 1991, in Operation Provide Comfort aiding Kurdish refugees in Northern Iraq.

Though I didn't fully know it then, Provide Comfort turned out to be a predictor and model for the new post–Cold War battlefields. It was also for me another major turning point: my first time conducting operations on one of these difficult, complex, new, and *different* battlefields—battlefields characterized by a bewildering multiplicity of unexpected dimensions. Provide Comfort made me realize that we would never again fight wars the old-fashioned way—like World War II, Korea, and even Vietnam—whose chief characteristic was the clash of organized military forces climaxed by big set-piece battles.

As I plunged into Provide Comfort, I found myself involved in day-to-day activities and actions that were not 99 to 100 percent military. Instead of a purely military focus, I was now exposed to political issues, economic issues, humanitarian issues, social issues, international agency issues, NGO issues, media issues. Most of these were outside military experience, doctrine, and training. We learned what we needed to know on the spot.

Yet it wasn't the issues themselves or their number that chiefly hit me out there, but their complexity, and how the complexity shot out and touched everything else. No event was isolated. Everything was intertwined.

⚎

In April 1991, even as we were celebrating the end of hostilities in the First Gulf War, the Kurdish crisis was brewing in northern Iraq. Amid all the euphoria, the rest of the world was giving little attention to the looming tragedy . . . until Secretary of State Baker heard about it and flew out to check the scene for himself. Hours later, EUCOM was ordered into action (we got the call because our base of operations would be in Turkey, which is in EUCOM's region and from which we had conducted a number of operations during the Gulf War). I was assigned a major role in the operation: in its early days, I was deputy commander; later, when it grew much larger, I became chief of staff.

When we arrived in Turkey, we were aware that we were not getting into a strictly textbook military operation, yet we saw a military mission and perspective that weren't difficult to grasp. The Kurdish people had rebelled against Saddam Hussein's tyranny; he'd cracked down, crushed the rebellion, and forced the Kurds to flee into the mountains. We now had to push back the Iraqis, protect the Kurds, and provide security for ourselves and the other aid givers. If Saddam's military didn't comply with our demands, our military response was clear.

At the start of the operation, we understood what we had to do and how to do it and were prepared for everything we expected on the ground. We had UN agencies, such as UNHCR (UN High Commission for Refugees); we had U.S. agencies, such as our Office of Foreign Disaster Assistance (OFDA); we had sixty non-governmental organizations (NGOs), such as Oxfam, CARE, and Doctors Without Borders; and a coalition of thirteen nations sent military forces. We expected we could handle all that.

The real complications came later.

Soon after we arrived, the humanitarian mission was added to our military one. We were asked to save lives as well as take care of security; the Kurds up in the mountains were in a traumatized state in extremely harsh conditions. People were living in makeshift tents and shelters. They were starving. Sanitation was appalling. Diseases were breaking out. Hundreds—maybe thousands—were dying.

Though humanitarian missions weren't a normal part of our toolkit, we understood how to deliver food, water, shelter, basic health care. We knew how to take care of peoples' immediate needs, and that's what we saw as our job: "Disaster hits; we feed them, stabilize them, and then we're done and we're out of here." We very quickly prepared and successfully launched that part of the operation.

What we weren't prepared for were the big, long-term political complexities we ran into. The more or less straightforward mission we thought we were getting grew into an alien and complex operation that bore scarce resemblance to any military operation in our experience. And the crisis we'd expected to handle "immediately" soon took on a bewildering array of dimensions requiring actions it would take us months—even years—to accomplish. We left behind a temporary solution of no-fly zones and security areas that remained in place for twelve years.

The Cultural Dimension

Kurds come in many forms; there were social differences, political differences, factions, tribes. Some Kurds were educated and sophisticated, others were not. Those from the towns and cities were less used to harsh conditions than those from the country. They had a harder time adapting to the rigors of mountain exile. These differences required careful and sensitive actions in several dimensions. A humanitarian rescue was not going to be a simple, one-note affair.

The Political and Diplomatic Dimensions

Our mission was the first I'd encountered in which we had a significant political and diplomatic component. It was not the last.

Our task force was assigned a political adviser (POLAD)—a State Department representative whose job was to advise the commander on sensitive political issues and policy positions. We also had a liaison team from the U.S. Embassy in Ankara headed up by the deputy chief of mission, the number two diplomat there. It was clear that this was not just a purely military operation and that sensitive political and diplomatic issues were going to figure heavily in our calculations.

Millions of Kurds live in northern Iraq; millions more live in southeastern Turkey; more millions live in Syria and Iran. All Kurds feel a strong ethnic and national identity and hope for a Kurdish nation—Kurdistan. For years, Kurdish terrorist groups like the PKK had caused unacceptable mayhem in Turkey. Fearing a destabilizing Kurdish presence in Turkey, the Turks had a rigid position on handling the Kurds spilling over from Iraq. Essentially: no way. Our very presence inside Turkey and every aspect of our mission were sensitive. Our embassy in Ankara had to negotiate a modus vivendi with the Turks that provided us with enough freedom of action to do our job. In the end, the Turks accepted our presence, but we clearly made them very nervous.

On the southern side of the Turkish-Iraqi border, we had to keep the Iraqi military in line. In order to prevent confrontation while forcing them to back off, we had to set up a military coordination center—another difficult and complex interaction. We were not there to defeat Saddam's armies—that had already been done; our effort was to accomplish our mission without a military confrontation, and for the most part, we succeeded in that goal (though we ran into a few dicey situations with the Iraqis). The war was over in the south; the Iraqis were not eager to take us on in the north.

The Kurds had their own military and political system. Their militias were called the *peshmerga*—"those who face death"—tough and battle-hardened guerrilla warriors. Man for man they were more than a match for Saddam's soldiers. How friendly were they going to be? Would they cooperate? Or would they put up obstacles?

The two chief political parties were the Kurdish Democratic Party (KDP), under Massoud Barzani, and the Patriotic Union for Kurdistan (PUK), under Jalal Talabani. While both sought Kurdish independence, each had its own approach and political agenda, and they had been rivals in the past.

We had no sense of who or what we were dealing with.

Meanwhile, the humanitarian disaster was growing worse. Everybody in the camps was desperate for food, water, and medicine. Children and the elderly were dying.

We obviously needed people up in the mountains to stabilize the refugee camps and coordinate with the Kurds—a logical mission for Special Forces, who are trained to interact with local populations. The entire 10th Special Forces Group (three battalions) under Colonel Bill Tangney came down from Europe and the United States and immediately went to work in the camps. When it was all over, the Green Berets had saved thousands of lives.

One of their first tasks was to look for leaders in the camps. We approached the people we'd normally talk to first: lawyers, doctors, English speakers, and the Western educated. These professionals did not have the authority or influence to get things done. Next we looked for political leaders—like the PUK and KDP leaders—with not much greater success. The political leaders were not tribal leaders. They occupied a different place in the Kurdish scheme.

As we were struggling through these obstacles, blessed help came to us in the person of Nelgun Nesbit, a tough, outspoken army officer whom I already knew from EUCOM. A native Turk (her father was a Turkish general) who had immigrated to the United States, Nell had joined our army and become an intelligence officer. She spoke both Turkish and Kurdish. "General Zinni," she explained, "you need to understand the Kurds' social system. We're trying to connect with them in ways that don't suit their culture. You're going to the wrong people"—a point we were already starting to understand. "You're thinking like a Westerner," she continued. "The Kurds are a tribal society. They listen most to their tribal chiefs."

She then found me a Kurdish schoolteacher who laid out everything needed to understand Kurdish society: the tribes, the political system, the decision makers—and she explained how and where to find the tribal chiefs, the elders or "agas."

The leaders we'd worked so hard to find had all the time been doing what they'd been doing for countless generations, sitting on rugs at the back of their tents holding court. The Special Forces troops then set out to do what they are trained so well to do: they squatted down on the rugs, ate goat with the agas, and got friendly. This put us through the door; greater cooperation followed.

The Coalition Dimension

Even back in 1991, we'd had considerable experience working with coalition militaries. We knew how to organize and structure coalitions so everyone cooperated and coordinated.

Yet, certain issues have to be worked out in every coalition operation—military interoperability issues, rules of engagement issues, accountability issues, political issues, technical issues (such as communications interoperability: we had to bring in sixteen short tons of military communications equipment to assure communications with everybody), cultural issues, and even friction points.

In a coalition, we had different levels of military control. The U.S.-led task force might have tactical control of a unit from country X; or it might have operational control; or it might have actual command (in the case of U.S. forces). Tactical control means that I can only give the unit tactical direction within an agreed-upon mission. Operational control means I can change their mission (some countries weren't open to this). Command means just that. Some forces came with political limitations on what they could do or what missions they could accept. So when we did the planning, we had to make sure that officers from all the participating nations were integrated into the coalition staff.

Our solutions to these problems produced some weird relationships, and we often had to improvise and kluge them together to make them work.

At one point General Colin Powell—who was then chairman of the Joint Chiefs of Staff—came out to look over the operation. During my briefing with him, I showed him a nice chart we had carefully produced to show command relationships. It had all kinds of lines of authority that appeared more direct and neat than the actual situation. General Powell, a very astute human being, obviously saw that the reality wasn't as clean as the chart. He looked at me and laughed: "What are the command relationships here? Is it OPCON? TACON?" (Operational Control, Tactical Control).

I shuffled my feet, and said, "Sir, it's HANDCON. We're doing much of this on a handshake."

He loved it. He turned to our commander, General John Shalikashvili: "This is excellent! This is reality! You're flexible. You adapt. You find a way to work out agreement. That's got to be the way it's got to be done to get on with the critical mission." General "Shali" was an expert at gaining coalition support and working around sticky political issues that hampered military cooperation.

The NGO Dimension

Back when I was a colonel, I had no idea what an NGO was. I'd never heard of the beast.

Today, any colonel in the military knows what an NGO is. He has probably worked with them. Even if he hasn't, he will know how effectively they deliver aid, health care, food, shelter, clean water, and all the other necessities of life to people at great risk, often in conditions of great danger. NGOs have long since proved themselves to be necessary and indispensable. Some jobs only they can do well.

My first encounter with NGOs was in Operation Provide Comfort. It was not a totally smooth encounter, but together we made it work.

In a sense, NGOs are miniature nations. Each has a more or less unique culture. Each has a specific mission. Each has a history. Each has rules, a standard of conduct, a charter, and a mission statement under which it operates. So in many ways working with NGOs requires the kind of cultural sensitivity needed to work with foreign peoples or alien cultures. You have to understand and appreciate their culture and make yourself sensitive to the many dimensions that your culture and theirs do *not* share. You have to see what they do, how they're structured to do it, and why they are the way they are.

Most NGO workers are honorable and well intentioned . . . wonderful human beings. That doesn't make them always easy to take.

I used to joke that whenever I met NGO workers we automatically came from opposing cultures: Here is a young woman, maybe just out of college, in sandals, jeans, and a "Save the Whales" T-shirt. And here am I in my Michelin Man Kevlar flak jacket and helmet, weapon, and all kinds of other military equipment hanging from me. Right away, she's talking to her father, and I'm talking to my daughter. Right away we've got a problem. I'm telling her things she doesn't want to hear. She's telling me things I don't want to hear, and in *ways* I don't want to hear. It's not just that she disagrees with me, she's got a suspicious attitude that gets under my skin. My military attitude gets under hers. I'm John Philip Sousa and she's Joan Baez. Harmony will be tough.

We have no choice but to bridge our differences. In operations like Provide Comfort, they needed us and we needed them.

Practically, that meant working out on the spot and for the first time systems that allowed the military and NGO cultures to coexist (systems that proved effective enough to use later in other humanitarian missions). That wasn't easy . . . not with organizations that are so different.

NGOs come in a bewildering variety. Sixty NGOs on the ground will mean sixty different organizations. Unlike the military, there's no center. No mother ship.

Some organizations are nationally based; some are international. Some are secular; some are religion-affiliated. They come with different missions: some focus on water; some on shelter; some on medical care; some on capacity building—setting up institutions such as education systems, health care systems, or legal systems.

Sometimes those with similar missions compete with one an-other. Medical care NGOs might, for instance, set up shop in the same area to perform similar roles rather than finding locations where they can each do good.

NGOs all compete for donations.

They cherish their independence. They like minimal structure, and they don't like doctrine or rules. They like flexibility and to be free to think and act according to the situation. And they resist attempts to be hammered into a single organization.

We weren't just facing questions about different—and some-times opposing—cultures. We had policy issues. We had operational level issues. We had nitty-gritty coordination issues. We ran into all kinds of different charters. The charter of the International Commit-tee of the Red Cross requires the Red Cross to maintain strict neu-trality. They cannot be seen as working with the military, because doing that would create the perception that they had taken a side or a position. We had to respect that. Yet, I had to understand that Red Cross workers have needs that only we can meet. There has to be some level of coordination.

The military may bring emergency capacities at scales and speeds that NGOs can't begin to approach; the NGOs bring a depth of un-derstanding of the needs, requirements, and capacities for long-term recovery that we don't have.

The NGOs complain that the military, with its monolithic and structured perspective, misses the subtleties of humanitarian aid and its aftermath. In their view, we set up systems that are not trans-ferable, and we make the people we're trying to help too dependent on the aid we provide. The NGOs have a different approach. They start with humanitarian aid: you have to save lives at risk. But then you have to move to what they call "sustainment" as quickly as pos-sible. The idea is to leave behind systems that the people themselves can operate. "Don't give them fish," the saying goes, "Teach them how to fish."

The Kurdish refugees in the mountains desperately needed pure water. The military can come in and set up ROWPU units—Reverse Osmosis Water Purification Units—and start pure water flowing right away. But when the military leaves, the ROWPU units leave with them. By way of contrast, an organization like Oxfam can come in and set up more sustainable systems that will operate after they have left. (One of Oxfam's specialties is setting up water systems.)

We ran into similar questions over medical care. The military brought in world-class medical care facilities—far better than the Kurds had known back home. Doctors Without Borders and others came in with a less sophisticated approach to health care, but one that the Kurds could maintain.

The NGOs need to operate within a secure environment to be most effective; and we want them to be safe. And yet many of them— like the Red Cross—are proscribed from a "close" relationship with us. Others want to be protected, but refuse to accept the constraints or association that implies. How do we square those circles?

Sometimes all we can do is keep them informed about where we are operating, what we're doing, and what's safe and unsafe. But if we can, we share intelligence and information. We try to create secure areas for them to operate in.

The frictions and the resentments between the military and NGOs turn both ways.

When the Kurdish crisis burst into the media, Americans back home mobilized—as Americans always do—and collected money and clothes: "We've got to help the Kurds. We'll collect boxes of sweaters."

That was wonderful and generous. But then we had to handle all those boxes of sweaters when they arrived in Turkey and funnel them through very limited airfields.

Suddenly some aircraft would appear overhead, unannounced and low on fuel, and demand to be allowed to land. Where could we put it? We already had military planes on the ground, and we already had scheduled relief supplies backed up. We didn't have room for them. But we couldn't make them turn back; they were running out of gas. So they'd land, and we would learn that the aircraft had been contracted by some volunteer organization back in the States to bring in boxes of sweaters—all un-palletized. We didn't need sweaters; the Kurds had no use for them, since they were not cold. Now these perfectly well-meaning folks had blocked up military support planes on the ground and planes carrying food that the Kurds were desperate for. Since the sweaters weren't on pallets and the folks on the plane didn't have the means to offload the sweaters, we either had to send over our materiel-handling equipment—fork lifts—or offload them by hand.

After we had taken care of all that, the representatives from the charitable organization would demand assurances that the sweaters would safely reach the Kurds. And we'd have to tell them, "No, that's not going to happen. The Kurds don't need sweaters. The priority is food and medicine. They have enough shelter and clothing."

And they'd say, "What do you mean? We collected these sweaters. Now you have to deliver them." Then they'd go off filled with righteous outrage at the incompetence of the military.

A day or two later, the charity would get their people on a TV morning show and complain: "We collected clothing for the suffering Kurds. And when we brought it out there, at great expense, our military gave us a hard time. Here we are trying to do good, but our military can't get their act together."

I can't fault the obviously fine intentions of any organization that sacrificed time and money to help the Kurds. But we were running a vast and complex operation with limited resources through a very limited infrastructure. It does no good to arrive unannounced and expect instant service, no matter how well intentioned you are.

Contrast this with the way the Red Cross handles international emergencies: "Give us money," they advise. "Don't give us clothes or food. We know where to find clothes and food. And we know how to prioritize bringing everything in. But bringing it in helter-skelter clogs the system."

I came away from Provide Comfort with the realization that NGOs were new partners on the battlefield and we needed to learn how to work together. Both the military and the NGOs knew that we had to find some way to end our frictions and resentments—or at least to minimize them. I began to ask myself and others, How do we do that? Do we merely de-conflict? That is, ease frictions? Do we go farther and pass information back and forth? Can we actually coordinate with them on some level? Or do we simply end up in a dilemma and let nature take its course?"

We had the very complex challenge of finding a bridge between a very structured organization and a herd of cats (to borrow a metaphor from a friend, former Assistant Secretary of State Chester Crocker).

As always, personalities are key. In northern Iraq we had for the most part the right mix of personalities—people who were seriously engaged in problem solving and who wanted to cooperate and make it work.

But a couple of the wrong kinds of personalities is all it takes to gum up the system. (In Somalia, as I saw later on, there were too many conflicting personalities, too many people who didn't see what had to be done in the same way.)

In northern Iraq, we started by setting up unthreatening people-to-people links—liaison teams—with the NGOs. We later came up with the idea of creating a venue for airing out our friction points and differences and sharing ideas and plans. We expected at the least to minimize frictions, but perhaps also to generate some measure of cooperation, if not coordination. Since NGOs want to determine for themselves where they should go and what they should do, and don't want to submit themselves to a master plan—especially one controlled by the military—we tried to create an unstructured yet cooperative system. The venue we created was called the Civil-Military

Operations Center (CMOC in military jargon). CMOC, which was run by our Civil Affairs officers, provided a forum for solving problems with NGOs.

Learning how to cross-communicate with the NGOs and build a level of coordination and cooperation required a tremendous amount of work. That was the most important function of the CMOC. But even then—looking back at the way we have to approach all cultures—we always had a deeper goal: "Let me understand what you do. Who are you? What do you do? How do you do it? How can I help you? How can you help me?"

Northern Iraq saw the first use of the Civil-Military Operations Center as the clearinghouse where Civil Affairs could interact with NGOs. Later on we used CMOCs in Somalia and Haiti (though in Somalia they had to be adapted to conditions that were far more complex than those in northern Iraq). Now they have become doctrinally accepted and are the basis for other innovations currently in place.

A few years later, for example, when I commanded the First Marine Expeditionary Force (I MEF), I began a training and education program called Emerald Express that was designed to specifically address military participation in these kinds of operations. I wanted to bring "muddy boots" practitioners together with policymakers and planners. I invited many NGOs to attend and participate. It was vital, in my mind, for the NGOs and the military to understand each other and develop the structures and procedures to work with each other on these new battlefields. Emerald Express produced solid results; and we have made significant progress since then, but we still have a long way to go.

Mary McClymont, the president of Interaction, an association of U.S. NGOs, recently met with me to discuss issues she intended to raise with the Joint Staff regarding NGO–military humanitarian work in Afghanistan. Among the issues she brought up was the military's practice of wearing civilian clothes while conducting humanitarian tasks (like distributing food). It was clear to me that the military probably did this to present a less-intimidating image and to encourage Afghans to accept the aid. But to the NGOs this blurred the lines between military and civilians and put them at risk. They wanted a clear distinction between military personnel and aid workers.

This is a classic example of a well-intentioned act that produces confusion or misinterpretation. It is also an example of the need to take into account all the potential ramifications. This kind of understanding can only be gained by cooperation and communication.

The Humanitarian Dimension

In military operations, we are trained to take into account factors that directly affect the accomplishment of the military mission, such as weather, terrain, enemy forces, and friendly forces. In operations like Provide Comfort, new and unfamiliar factors were thrown into the mix of traditional ones in our estimate of the situation. As an example, the Centers for Disease Control (CDC) provided critical input, as did medical personnel in charge of preventive medicine. We also had to handle refugees, which required special processes and procedures we were not familiar with.

By the time winter had turned to spring, we had stabilized the camps; everyone in the mountains had enough to eat; and we were getting a handle on the health crises. But we still had hundreds of thousands of Kurdish refugees in the mountains. "What do we do with them?" we asked.

Predictably, we took a short-range view: "Okay, we've got half a million refugees on the Iraq-Turkey border. The Turks don't want them there. Once we've stabilized them up in the mountains, we'll take a small slice of northern Iraq, build nice, semipermanent refugee camps there—large enough to accommodate all of them— and make life better for them."

The UN refugee organization had zero enthusiasm for that idea. The UNHCR, which deals with millions of refugees around the world, had learned one big lesson over better than fifty years of experience: no permanent camps, no permanent refugees. Keeping people refugees forever does them no favors, and their presence (whether they are tolerated or despised) is a nightmare for everyone involved—as Palestinian experience has long demonstrated.

We started building camps just the same, in a valley on the Iraq side of the border. That would at least solve immediate problems: it would take the refugees out of Turkey and put them on Kurdish territory that much closer to their real homes. But sending them back to their actual homes would require removing the Iraqi army from Kurdish territories, possibly by force, and Washington was not yet ready for that.

Typically, the camps we built were comfortable; we wanted to make sure we provided for every need. The U.S. military knows how to build great camps.

The UN came back to us: "Stop," they said, "this is wrong. It won't work. We don't want more camps, not even in Iraq. We want to *un-refugee* them. You've got to get these people home!

"But if you have to build camps," they continued, "make them temporary. Make them austere. Make them meet only basic needs. Discourage the people from staying." They were right on all counts, but we didn't yet completely understand all they were telling us.

Our next hurdle was to persuade the Kurds to move down into these camps. Since most of them were still traumatized by the terrors that had driven them into the mountains in the first place, few wanted to risk leaving apparent safety.

But we knew that if we could turn the agas around, the other Kurds would follow. We tried showing videos. The tribal leaders remained unconvinced. We then suggested sending a delegation of young men down to check the camps out personally; and the agas bought that.

Of course, the camps we built were military camps—all straight lines and grids and orderly, with great sightlines. We took the delegation down to the camps; they looked them over and shook their heads: "This is all very nice," they told us. "But it won't work. We just don't live that way." Kurds don't like nice, straight, military rows. They like their communities and neighborhoods to focus on the clan and tribal centers, in little inward-turning cul-de-sacs.

We redesigned the camps. The Kurds accepted the changes and agreed to move.

By this time, we had begun to realize that the UN had been right all along: We couldn't get a little bit pregnant. The camps we'd made were not a permanent solution. "That's not enough," the UNHCR kept insisting. "Let them go *home*. We admit it's a big job. You've got to transport half a million people down the mountains. The roads are primitive and dangerous"—some little better than trails or paths next to precipitous drops—"while many Kurds still suffer from the terrors that drove them up there in the first place. You may not be able to achieve the move in a single leap. But if you have to set up camps to house them, don't make them comfortable. You have to give the people the clear message that the camps are temporary. It's a carrot and stick thing. You have to leave a trail of bread crumbs leading them back home."

The reverse side to that coin was the Iraqi military occupation of Kurdish territories.

Taking the Kurds back home meant pushing the Iraqis out and setting up a security zone in northern Iraq. That was not going to sit well with the government in Baghdad, and we had no guarantee that they would not make a stand there and fight. Though we'd certainly fight them if we had to, we preferred intimidation. Either way, throwing Iraqi forces out of northern Iraq would require beefing up our own forces.

Our officers in northern Iraq meanwhile set up a liaison with the *peshmerga,* and set up good connections with Barzani, Talibani, and their political organizations. These contacts proved very useful during the coming weeks.

We got what we wanted from the Iraqis in the end, but not without stresses and strains and tense moments. The Iraqis didn't yield Kurdish territory easily or gracefully.

A New Role for the Military

I returned to Stuttgart in November of 1991, seven months after I'd left for Provide Comfort. By then I'd come to realize that I'd been engaged in more than just a strange kind of military operation. It was a radically changed kind of military operation—a "military" operation in which the combat military was no longer the centerpiece of the operation, the main effort. And it was a military operation requiring "military" responses to a multiplicity of dimensions never before faced by the military.

The mission in northern Iraq quickly proved to be anything but an aberration. We would see these missions again and again. In accomplishing them, we found ourselves confronting again and again the new face of war. It was a far cry from war as we had previously known it.

The military struggled with these missions over the next decade . . . even as the military tool became the only instrument our nation seemed to be willing to throw at the growing problems of instability. The military is a very powerful tool, but it has limits.

It knew how to deal with the security dimension of the problems it faced; but it was increasingly saddled with the political, humanitarian, reconstruction, social, economic, and other dimensions. In several cases, the military did not give these other dimensions the kind of emphasis it was able to put on building and maintaining security; the military had a disproportionate responsibility for dimensions it was not capable of supporting. The military was asked to fill voids it was not designed to fill.

Employment of the military in these missions became controversial. The Weinberger and Powell Doctrines of the mid-1980s for committing the military, born out of the lessons of Vietnam, did not seem to cover the demands of these new missions. According to these doctrines, there had to be a vital national interest at stake before we could commit our military. We had to commit to "win"; we had to have a clear objective; we had to have support from both Congress and the people; we needed a clear exit strategy; we needed to use overwhelming force; and the military action had to come as a last resort. These doctrines seemed to be a recipe for World War II type commitments.

At a dinner with Secretary of State Madeleine Albright, at which several generals and admirals were invited to discuss these new challenges, she posed this question, "How do you commit the military to missions with limited objectives, limited political will, and limited resources?" I knew what she meant. She was asking how we understood war. Could we operate only from the old, conventional models—quickly growing obsolete? Or could we understand and operate in the new environment?

In the military we understood total war. We knew unconditional surrender. We understood response to an attack on us or our vital interests. Our understanding of war and warfare, our very thought processes about fighting and combat, all had their origins in a single model—World War II. The "good war" had in many ways formed our standards for employment of the military and for military operations. These confusing and messy new missions didn't fit that model.

Meanwhile, the world was getting more messy and confused. Secretary Albright's question demanded an answer.

THE NEW FACE OF WARFARE

Since the fall of the Soviet empire, something like forty wars have broken out around the world. Few of these have been wars as Americans generally understand them—nation(s) against nation(s), massed mechanized encounters of force upon force; big set-piece battles; the advance on and capture of the enemy capital; peace treaties followed by victory parades. These new wars are smaller in scale; contending forces are usually irregular; weapons are usually light; violence is brutal; the old conventions and rules rarely apply; civilians suffer the greatest proportion of casualties; progress is hard to measure and victory hard to define; and fighting occurs in parts of the world few Americans can easily find on a map—in Africa, in Asia, parts of Latin America, the Middle East.

Communist insurgencies of the twentieth century, inspired and designed by Lenin, Mao, and Che Guevara, laid the foundations for sophisticated asymmetric warfare that allowed militarily inferior forces to confront and confound more powerful, modern military forces. The enemies we face today learned from these experiences. They now leverage tactics, technology, and popular discontent to accomplish their aims.

These new conflicts are worrying. But they are only one component of the new dangers we are facing; they *may* have a violent component; but the violence is never their only component, or even necessarily the most important one. The new dangers are not neat or clear. They come with a complex and confusing tangle of political, religious, economic, ethnic, cultural, health, and environmental components—all of them playing out on battlefields where there is only scattered violence, or even no overt violence.

World War II defined America for the twentieth century, just as our Revolution defined America at our nation's birth, and our Civil War defined America in the next century. World War II marked our entrance onto the world stage as a great nation and a world leader. We had encountered nothing like it before in our history.

How do we account for its impact on our national soul?

Unlike any war we've fought before or since, we had moral clarity . . . a clarity that was classically American in its expression of who we believe we are. We weren't threatening anybody. We didn't build up our military to conquer. We were attacked. The evil nature of our attackers was clear. They were responsible for this dastardly blow. They broke the rules.

Our nation was mobilized and united. We built up from nothing. We went across the seas and drove our forces into the heart of the enemy. We pursued unconditional surrender. And we did it. We defeated the enemy fair and square. He admitted defeat; he capitulated completely. And then we reached down, picked him up, and rebuilt his society into something magnificent.

And we had heroes—Audie Murphy, Ernie Pyle, the men at D-Day, a "Band of Brothers," our "Greatest Generation."

It was the right cause. We were all pulling for the nation; the nation came together. It was nice; it was clean; it was good. The Good War—the model for the way wars ought to be.

The trouble is, the model fit World War II and not the conflicts of the rest of the century.

All the wars we've fought after World War II—Korea, Vietnam, Afghanistan, Iraq—have been nothing like that war. Neither were our other military involvements, such as Somalia or Haiti. Neither were the wars we fought before World War II, like the Banana Wars we fought in the Caribbean in the 1920s and 1930s, or the guerrilla war we had fought earlier in the Philippines.

That didn't matter. We ignored all that. War on the World War II model became a metaphor for anything tough and serious that Americans take on. Americans don't work to eliminate poverty or to reduce poverty. We declare war on poverty. We declare war on illiteracy; war on crime; war on drugs; war on terror. The World War II mindset influences every large-scale task the nation undertakes.

Our World War II experience became the model for how we organized our military forces. It became the model for how we expected conflicts to unfold. It became the model for major combat operations. It became the model for how we looked at enemies.

When we want to engage in conflicts like Iraq and Vietnam, we must have a cause. We must have somebody to attack us. We must have bad guys we can demonize. Our leaders cooked up the Gulf of Tonkin incident to justify our war in Vietnam. Our leaders cooked up Saddam Hussein's secret weapons of mass destruction and collaboration schemes with Al Qaeda to justify our war in Iraq. We had to cook up the rationale. We had to follow the model.

We then expect to define victory our way. The bad guys have to follow the rules as we understand them. And they have to admit defeat when we say they're beaten, when we've defeated their uniformed military forces.

It hasn't worked out that way. Few wars or military interventions since World War II have had complete or satisfying conclusions. Unlike World War II, we have left these battlefields with outcomes we don't like, or at best with only partial or temporary resolutions.

The old set of rules—under which military forces met in uniform on a battlefield in accordance with the Geneva Convention—described a very stylistic form of warfare that was practiced well into the twentieth century. Warriors who fought on the field of battle and shed honorable blood might have an awareness of political issues, cultural issues, moral issues, economic issues, or historical issues, but such issues didn't pollute the pure conduct of the fight.

The old idealistic and rules-based warfare is now gone. It has morphed and melded into all sorts of other messy dynamics. You can't separate the political, cultural, historical issues from the honorable blood that's shed on the battlefield. Now, a military professional has to understand all these other dimensions of war, and how his or her particular piece of the action fits into the totality of the effort.

Today, if the United States takes some kind of military action, its effects shoot out beyond the military dimension. If the United States conducts a military operation to root out insurgents in some village, what we do to the tribe members who live in the village could alienate them. But if we choose another way to root out the insurgents, we might build confidence in the tribe and bring them over to our side.

In Somalia, the Marines were running an operation in an area called Kismayo, where we had a lot of problems. The Marine commander called from a village: "We've surrounded a mosque where we believe there are weapons. As we started to enter it, the imam blocked the door. 'You can't enter that mosque,' he told us. 'If you do, there's going to be hell to pay.'"

"Tell him to wait a minute," I said, "until we can talk to some of our Muslim troops" in our coalition. "Tell him we'll fly down a Muslim platoon, and they will go into the mosque."

The commander explained all this to the imam. And a few minutes later, the commander called me: "The imam says that if you're willing to do that, he's willing to let us into the mosque. But what he's asking is that we don't go storming inside. He'll take me and a few others in there to show me there's no weapons, and he'll let us search all we want."

And that's what happened. They found a single AK–47.

The gesture of respect for the culture and religion was enough to solve the problem.

Any military professional who fails to understand the subtle levels of such dynamics will fail to accomplish the missions our military faces today. Or else he or she will simply repeat Vietnam: "Just kill enough enemies and we win." It doesn't work that way anymore.

Our current war in Iraq may be turning into a repetition of Vietnam. The military out there goes from operation to operation; our leaders in Washington assure us we are powering ahead from success to success; yet our young nineteen- or twenty-year-old soldiers are now asking hard questions: "I can win any battle. But am I winning this war?"

I've heard these questions before, in Vietnam. The answer there was "No."

My answer for Iraq is, "I don't know." Nobody can tell our soldiers if they're winning or not. But the parallels are disturbing.

The new warfare requires a new kind of warrior. It's no longer enough to be a good military officer, skilled in the arts of war. We need to broaden our education. We need renaissance men and women. We need officers who are part economist, part political scientist, part anthropologist, and part all sorts of other disciplines. It isn't enough just to be militarily savvy. We have to understand how that fits in the bigger picture. If I think that what I'm doing militarily—going out there and killing people and breaking things—is all there is basically to my job, then I don't understand my job.

A military unit that gets thrown into Iraq has to understand who are the Shia, the Sunni, the Kurds, the Chaldeans, the Turcomans, the Syrians; they have to understand tribes and their relationships to other tribes; they have to understand history.

When I was in Somalia, the Somalis kept attacking Egyptian and Nigerian troops. We had to figure out why. It turned out that the Somalis hated the Nigerians because they had given sanctuary to the deposed evil dictator, Siad Barre; Barre was in exile in Nigeria.

It turned out that the Egyptians were hated because of a very popular conspiracy theory among Somalis. According to this theory, the Egyptians had cut a deal with Siad Barre to move a million Egyptians from southern Egypt to take over the Juba Valley and drive Somali farmers out of the most fertile lands of Somalia.

What did that mean for me? It meant we had to take these situations into account when we made military decisions. "Where do I place our Nigerian or Egyptian troops, here, or here?" They obviously had to go where frictions with Somalis could be kept to a minimum.

In the twenty-first century we may find ourselves engaged in con-flicts where there is no exchange of violence. An enemy may attack our information systems. An enemy may undermine our economic systems. An enemy may use worldwide information networks to dis-credit us, create suspicion and hatred, and promote violence against us. Violence against us may not come directly from our enemies but from those our enemies inflame.

Even those adversaries who choose to engage with us in a violent conflict are not going to step out in the center ring and fight "fair and square." We're too big. We're too powerful. We start with too many advantages. Fighting us our way guarantees our victory.

What will they do? They'll come at us in an asymmetric fash-ion. They're not going to play by the rules. They're not going to face our strengths—tanks on tanks, artillery on artillery, air on air. They will hit us where we are most vulnerable. We're going to find our-selves fighting on battlefields that are much more murky than we like. We're going to see tactics that don't play to our strengths—ter-rorism, insurgencies, civil wars, and other messy businesses. They may attack with anthrax or plague; they may attack the environ-ment; they may attack databases and other repositories of informa-tion. They may cut off our oil supply, or grab control of vital re-sources, to deny them to us. They may attack our quality of life in ways we cannot now imagine.

When I commanded CENTCOM, we threatened major air at-tacks against Iraq to force the Iraqi government to comply with conditions they had agreed to at the end of the first Gulf War. More than once they did not back down, and we had to carry out the attacks.

As deadlines approached, tensions with Iraq would mount. We would deploy some forces, move some airplanes, show some muscle. Though we had not yet fired a shot, we were showing Saddam the moves that he knew well would be preparatory to our launching an attack.

As we made our preparations, my J-6—my communications officer, my information systems manager—would come to me: "Sir, today we've had 1220 hits on our computer systems; up 640 hits from yesterday."

Whenever tensions with Iraq mounted, all my computer systems got increasing numbers of hits from hackers. Was this the work of sixteen-year-old kids from Munich? Maybe.

👀

The Department of Defense, aware that the world has changed (though I don't believe they yet understand how), has been reworking their definitions of military operations. They've come up with three categories. Let's look first at the two they clearly understand:

1. Major Combat Operations. That is, "War" as it is normally understood.
3. Military Support Activities. That is, "Engagement" as the Clinton administration understood it—training, military support activities, and the like.

And then there's the large muddy glob in the middle with no consistencies that allow definition:

2. This category ranges all over the place from humanitarian missions to peacekeeping to peace enforcement to minor conflicts that border on the edge of war or major operations. The Pentagon thinkers understand now the broad nature of these conflicts and they see that these have more than one dimension; but they have trouble finding ways to neatly categorize them.

At one time the Pentagon called these actions MOOTW. Next the term of art became Security and Stability Operations (SASO). Now they're called Irregular Operations. They can't decide on a name that fits the situation. They understand a *regular* operation. That's war that follows the World War II model—*real* war. Then there are all kinds of actions with other-than names—actions that are *other than* war—messy, nasty businesses like insurgencies, peace operations, complex, emergency humanitarian operations. These don't fit World War II–type major conventional operations, the end of the violence spectrum that we have so masterfully prepared for and dominated.

Though we must change the way we see and understand conflict, and that vision will inevitably bring changes to the ways we "fight" these conflicts, some characteristics of the way we fight won't change because they are so deeply embedded in American values and American character.

First, we are casualty sensitive. Our troops are never cannon fodder. We never believe in dominating a battlefield with mass formations of expendable troops. We do everything in our power to minimize deaths and injuries to our troops and to innocents.

Second, we are technology oriented. Because we want to minimize casualties, we use our technology to dominate the battlefield; and we want to leverage technology for all we can get out of it.

Third, we like expanded battlefields. We like to control the tempo of operations; we like to throw so many things at the enemy, that he can't cope. We not only expand the battlefield physically in size, in tempo, and in depth, but we want to expand it with alliances and information (psyops) campaigns.

Fourth, we want short duration conflicts with a clear moral superiority in our cause, total popular support, and specifically articulated objectives. We don't like protracted conflicts with murky objectives and popular confusion over our cause and justification.

The Pentagon leadership in the current Bush administration came into office with the intention of conducting a much overdue "transformation" of the military. Though transformation was—and is—needed, they saw the change as requiring high-tech solutions. In their thinking, ground units could be cut to pay the bills for advanced intelligence and communications systems and for sophisticated precision weapons. Some talk floating out of the five-sided labyrinth called for only a few lightly armed and manned gendarmerie units to police the battlefield after high technology decided the fight. I guess if all of our problems could simply be reduced to target points on which you could easily focus your cross-hairs, this might have worked. But the world is far from that simple.

Now that same Pentagon has an even newer vision. They want increases in ground unit strengths in the U.S. Army and Marine Corps, and they want to create a new doctrine for "Irregular Warfare."

The Pentagon leaders face the two-headed problem of preparing for the conceivable rise of a peer competitor to challenge us—such as China, or a China-Russia alliance—and the need for forces capable of operating in those irregular commitments. They face the dilemma of two widely different military requirements. Resources are obviously limited. Do we accept risk and primarily prepare for one? Do we build two military forces? Can we afford that? Do we relegate the irregular operations to a secondary or additional duty role and muddle along?

Tough questions.

We do not live in our grandfathers' world. And we cannot have our grandfathers' military. We basically retain a shrunken version of the Cold War military that is in dire need of an innovative transformation. We can't meet today's challenges with the force design, doctrine, training, equipment, and leader education of the past century.

CHAPTER FIVE

COLLIDING WORLDS

For most of history, inequality was tolerated because continents were separated by huge distances and characterized by cultural remoteness. In a world that has become proximate and more intimate, inequality is becoming less tolerable. How that rejection of inequality will be expressed depends, however, on whether it acquires a defined sense of direction and an accepted leadership.

—Zbigniew Brzezinski, 1993

For Americans, the United States is the City on the Hill. We live in a land blessed by never-ending progress, ever more amazing technological advances, and ever-expanding frontiers. Prosperity grows so unfailingly that we blithely overlook dips in the job and housing markets . . . they're inconsequential. The last significant economic depression is now a memory only among our eldest citizens. And a downturn worse than a depression? Inconceivable. A total collapse of *our* society? Unimaginable . . . except in movies. In movies we anxiously experience colossal world-shattering events—nuclear holocausts, comet strikes, breath-takingly sudden environmental catastrophes, knowing they're only happening on the screen. An ice age that rolls down overnight might look scary and exciting in a movie, but it won't happen here.

Absent such unlikely events, could an American civilization (or a European civilization, for that matter) collapse into a lawless world of rape, pillage, and looting, overseen—if you can call it that—by roving bands of armed criminal gangs and warlords backed by thuggish militias? No way. Our civilization is too solid and too strong, our systems and institutions too flexible and too protected by overlapping safety nets.

In America and the rest of the developed world we tend to take for granted our benign environment and our safety nets of stable and secure institutions. Security and stability feel so natural that few fear their loss. Bad things happen—earthquakes, floods, murders, drunk drivers plowing into schoolchildren—but afterward, order and security are quickly reestablished. We are confident that justice will be done. We feel protected; our systems work; and our level of expectation about the response to such events is very high. If some crazy rolls down the street shooting a gun, I pick up the phone and call 911. And I expect the police to come and take care of that problem. If a fire breaks out in my garage, I call and a fire truck comes. If a hurricane blasts all the roofs off and blows all the trees down, I expect FEMA, the state, and the county to clean up. And I am confident that the drunk who plowed into the kids will be punished.

As Americans or Europeans or Japanese, we don't give such things a second thought. Peace, security, stability, order, rule of law, a functioning infrastructure—these are all givens. They *seem* natural.

They are not natural.

Although Hurricane Katrina, which recently overwhelmed our shores along the Gulf of Mexico, shook our assumptions about all of this, our systems slowly recovered. We still enjoy and believe we have a level of security and stability that exceeds anything seen before in history . . . or anything that exists right now in most of the underdeveloped world.

The big difference between that world and ours: There the capacity to provide security, stability, and recovery is absent and the safety net is weak. Or it's missing. Instead of powerful systems that protect stability and order, we find disruptive systems that drive instability and disorder. Or else we find the absence of any system.

A functioning infrastructure? A functioning political system? A functioning justice and security system? A functioning finance and banking system? A functioning health system? A functioning food distribution system? A functioning disaster relief system? . . . Don't depend on it.

Their absence, together with their replacement by tangles of disruptive systems, provides the primary power source for generating conditions of instability.

Out in the field, I've been knocked over time and again by such instabilities. I've had a strange sense that two parallel worlds exist on this planet—a stable, progressively growing, developing world and an unstable, disintegrating, chaotic world. I've seen that second world up close and too often.

The Iraq–Turkey Border, 1991

When I was serving in Operation Provide Comfort—the coalition organized to save the Kurds that Saddam Hussein had driven into the mountain wilderness—the first thing that caught my attention was the breakdown of Kurdish society: The Kurds in the mountains had no security, no order, no sanitation, no systems for delivering food, just makeshift shelter. Half a million people lived in conditions of near total disorder, incapable of following the simple procedures needed to prevent cholera and other diseases. The Kurds were not primitive people; they could easily follow such simple procedures under normal conditions, but they were overwhelmed by the collapse of their normal structures. The best they could do was try to survive.

These people had no level of expectation, no safety net. There was nobody to call when the raping and pillaging began. There was nobody to call when the Iraqi army drove them out of their homes and into the mountain wastelands and slaughtered them with their artillery and aircraft. There was nobody to call when the Turks forced them to remain in the freezing mountains. There was nobody to call when the food ran out and the cold hit. There was nobody to call for shelter. There was nobody to call when the children and old people started dying.

They didn't expect help when help came.

Somalia, 1992–1993

In December 1992, I was sent to Somalia as director of operations of Operation Restore Hope, a UN-authorized mission conducted by the U.S Marines I MEF (Marine Expeditionary Force). The day I arrived, I began to wonder how a working society can spiral into chaos.

When I flew into Mogadishu, I dropped into a wasteland "future" exactly like a postapocalypse movie. It was a shock. I had never realized how far a society could disintegrate in so short a time. I had never realized how fragile civilized society can be.

Though Somalia was not Europe, Japan, or America, it had been a going concern, reasonably structured with the standard government and commercial institutions. It had universities and technical schools; it had police, an economy, trade, banks.

This was still admittedly third-world Africa. The infrastructure was not strong. There was severe poverty. Most areas lacked clean water. Many Somalis did not have enough to eat. There were endemic diseases. Infant mortality rates were disturbing. But it was a society that managed. It was not different in most respects from other third-world societies.

But then the fragile Somali institutions took a series of nasty hits.

During the waning days of the Soviet empire, after suffering many years of corrupt, incompetent, and repressive rule under the military dictator Siad Barre, the country had lurched into civil war. Barre was driven from power . . . but at enormous cost. Hundreds of thousands of Somalis were killed in the fighting, hundreds of thousands of refugees abandoned the country, and hundreds of thousands of other Somalis perished from starvation or disease. Twenty-five percent of all the children—including fully half of those born after 1987—died as a consequence of the fighting. The millions of Somalis who remained at home lived more precariously than the Kurds on the wintry border ridges.

The removal of Barre did not end the civil war. Factions of warlord-led clans continued the conflict, which was fueled by floods of weapons left over from the zero-sum Cold War superpower game. By 1992, all the institutions and systems that support and protect civilization had disappeared. Anarchy and chaos were total. There was no security, no police, no system of justice. It was rule by the gun and gang warfare, and by what you can grab or gain or hold onto. By then, Somalia was so ravaged, wrecked, and dangerous that NGOs and other relief providers could not do their jobs. The original mission of Operation Restore Hope was to provide security for the relief providers.

We arrived at the ransacked and partially destroyed airport. Derelict planes and ripped-apart equipment were piled up everywhere. Some of the destruction came from the war, some from looting and pillaging. By then, much of what could be called an economy in Somalia was conducted in the form of looting, pillage, or salvage.

We flew by helicopter over bombed-out ruins that had once been a beautiful port city of wide avenues, tiled roofs, and beautiful villas, and set down in a wrecked, gutted, and looted U.S. Embassy. *Everything* had been ripped out, including the pipes, floor tiles, and electric wiring. Squatters occupied the nearby buildings. Dead bodies, dead animals, and abandoned, burnt-out vehicles were scattered about the streets. Piles of garbage were everywhere.

Driving through the city was like entering Stalingrad in 1942–43—bullet-pocked and bomb-holed walls, blast craters, and evidence of looting. Squatters had moved into those government or university buildings that were still standing. Armed gangs and militias roamed the streets, many of them in old pickup trucks with crew-served automatic weapons mounted on the beds. These were called "technicals," having gotten the name from relief agencies who'd hired out the gangs to provide security—financing them with "technical assistance." Ordinary people trying to go about their business looked skittish and frightened. Even simple, necessary daily tasks were fraught with dread.

Mogadishu lies near the equator; it was very hot that December. The stench of death filled the oppressive heat.

Driving down the wrecked, littered, and devastated streets, it began to sink in that the city's, and the nation's, collapse had not come after a nuclear attack or an environmental catastrophe. The people had done it to themselves. As Pogo so tellingly put it, "We have met the enemy and he is us."

Yugoslavia, 1991

In Europe itself, parts of the once solid nation that had been Yugoslavia fell into a chaos as total as Somalia's. Much of Bosnia and Kosovo were as devastated as Mogadishu. I was assigned to EUCOM at that time and involved in the planning for Operation Provide Promise, a humanitarian effort aimed at holding together the fragmenting artificial nation. We knew then that Provide Promise was likely to fail, and that Yugoslavia was almost certainly destined to blow apart. We were right.

𝄢

As the governments in Somalia and Yugoslavia broke down, their fragile national identities also failed. In Somalia, everyone drew together along clan lines. The clan identity emerged as central; the clans were the only remaining viable communities. In the Balkans, ethnic identities took on a similar role. Yugoslavs became Serbs, Croats, Muslims. Nobody today calls himself a Yugoslav.

When institutions and control fail, when no single power can dominate a society, what is left? Stripping away a very fragile national identity will drive people into the strongest remaining communal identity.

Warlords will then often claim authority over their own clans or ethnic groups. Warlords and their clans will compete with other warlords for the scraps of the country that remain. And the spiral into chaos spins ever more savagely and terrifyingly out of control.

In the developed world, our level of awareness of instabilities like those that existed in precollapse Somalia or in prefission Yugoslavia is normally very low. Nor are many of us aware of how—when unchecked—these instabilities lead to violence, the collapse of order, or other crises. And yet the resulting chaos in our globalized world is no longer likely to remain contained by local or regional borders. The effects of chaos boiling half a world away can spill over and reach anywhere. We have already seen on 9/11 how such effects can wash up on our shores.

The media constantly report conditions of instability throughout the world. Some of these will remain inside local borders; but the more dangerous threaten to worsen and roll tsunami-like across other nations or regions, and even touch our own heartland.

In Central and South America, graft, nepotism, racketeering, and corruption threaten the democratic progress of the past quarter century; they rot government institutions and impede economic development. The region's citizens are growing ever more disillusioned with their elected officials, who are proving as adept at treating government as their own personal property as the absolute rulers they replaced. In country after country, frustrations are growing ever more violent. Many citizens look longingly back at dictatorial rule: Better a dictator and a growing economy than democracy stained with stagnation and corruption.

In the early 1970s, while I was a captain commanding a company, our ship pulled into Port-au-Prince, Haiti, for some liberty time, the first U.S. Navy ship to sail into Haiti in decades. I remember my first impressions as I walked around the city. Though I wasn't there during any particular crisis, it was clear to me that this was a society on the edge. The nation was still ruled by the Duvalier family. It was rule by terror. Nothing was new. Everything was shabby. All the cars seemed to have been on the road for decades. Even the money was decades old; they used American currency. The worn-down coins seemed to have been around since the nineteenth century. The abject poverty of the Haitians and the blatant brutality and violence of the Tonton Macoutes (government security forces) were evident. Everywhere I looked, I got the sense that people were struggling to keep their heads above water. The slightest added weight would surely sink them. And when those additional destabilizing weights were added, many people chose a desperate survival option: they headed for their makeshift boats and rafts and steered north. The survivors of the voyage eventually washed up on our shores like so much flotsam and jetsam.

Such conditions can be found on every inhabited continent.

Conditions in places like the Darfur region of Sudan, where tens of thousands of men, women, and children have been driven out of their villages by government-supported thugs, and are now living with little food or water in makeshift government refugee camps or across the border in Chad. They look like sticks; they're dressed in rags. In Darfur, thousands of fathers, grandfathers, and adolescent boys have been led away and murdered. Thousands of girls and women have been raped.

Conditions in Islamic countries, where too many young middle-class college graduates who have no hope of getting jobs or of having a voice in their political systems turn their outrage against American "crusaders" by joining extremist groups. These predatory groups easily exploit the frustration and anger over political, economic, or social conditions to brainwash the vulnerable youths, rationalizing with twisted religious ideologies their horrific acts of violence against innocents.

Conditions in African countries, where oil or diamonds or cocoa finance "insurgencies" whose only aim is to continue looting.

Conditions in countries where half of those in the generations we in America call "X" and "Y" have AIDS.

Conditions of poverty, as I found in Somalia in 1993.

One of my jobs in Operation Restore Hope was to visit our coalition units outside Mogadishu. One day, I dropped by an Italian unit working in a Somali village way out in the bush.

"Could you get us some rope?" they asked.

"Rope? What do you need rope for?"

"We need to tie up dead animals and drag them out in the water, so we can attract crocodiles and kill them."

I thought this was some kind of sport.

"No," they said. "The villagers have to get their water from a stream full of crocodiles. The crocodiles killed a couple of kids. So we've got to clean out the area where the villagers draw their water."

It's easy to focus on the plight of the villagers. But hardly less obvious is the absence of a functioning safety net; the absence of a functioning infrastructure, the absence of a supportive environment, and the prevailing poverty.

In 1950, the underdeveloped parts of the world contained about twice the population of the developed world. By 2050, they will contain six times the developed world's population, with much of the increase coming in Afghanistan, Burkina Faso, Burundi, Chad, Congo, Democratic Republic of the Congo, East Timor, Guinea-Bissau, Liberia, Mali, Niger, Uganda, Nigeria, Ethiopia, Pakistan, and Bangladesh . . . all among the poorest nations on earth.

Poverty is a prime marker for violence and civil war. The twenty poorest states are the ones most likely to collapse into violence. Somalia is one of the poorest twenty. So are Afghanistan and Haiti. The chain linking the rope and the crocodiles, and the plight of villagers with violence, chaos, and crisis is not immediately apparent. But it's there.

INSTABILITY

What *generates* "instabilities"? How do they fuel the collapse of societies? How does the chain of events sparked by these crises end up affecting us?

Instabilities result from two components: a degraded or unsustainable environment and failing, incapable, or corrupt institutions. An unstable society cannot cope—because of internal or external environmental issues, because its institutions aren't strong enough to withstand the pressures that challenge it, or because of the interaction of both sources.

When the institutions of a society fail, or its environment can no longer sustain it, instability is generated, and the structures of the society begin to fall apart. People react to the disintegration in various ways. Some take advantage of the absence of controls and become predators. Others simply hunker down and try to survive. Those who can, migrate to safer places that offer better opportunities for themselves and their families. Others lash out in anger at those who they perceive to be responsible for their plight.

Institutions

A society is stable when its institutions are strong, viable, and enduring. They can handle stress and stand up under crises. Strong institutions are those that the people support. They have legitimacy in the eyes of the people because the people believe they are fair and just. We think of government, the courts, the police as important institutions serving and protecting us. We are willing to pay taxes, and do it honestly, because we expect to get good value in return. When a society blessed with strong institutions faces security challenges, economic challenges, social challenges, or environmental challenges (like droughts or hurricanes), its institutions will hold up under the stresses and pressures. They will adapt to the changes; they may bend; but they will put together programs that will take on the challenges and overcome them.

Even when government institutions fall down on the job, other elements of our society—networks of people, companies, religious groups, NGOs, and the like—are likely to chip in. For example, the outpouring of support that followed the government's screw-ups after Hurricane Katrina.

When the institutions that provide for stability (governmental, economic, social, religious) can't bear up under those pressures—when the institutions are destroyed or collapse or break down—then the standards, rules, and systems those institutions enforced and promoted disappear. Order collapses; disorder and instability increase; and if nothing is done to halt the downward spiral, anarchy and chaos will result.

The institution that probably best indicates a society that's stable, or that's moving toward stability, is a viable, growing, and increasingly prosperous middle class . . . while a middle class that's withering and fading into the lower class—as the oligarchs and elites grow more powerful and wealthy—is a clear sign of instability.

Environment

The second component of stability—or of instability—is a viable environment or its absence. I'm talking about environment not only in the sense of the totality of nature, but also in the narrower sense of the specific conditions in which people live, the wherewithal needed to provide for the population—economic well-being, health, food, security, education. The environment is a society's essential capital; it's the substance of what makes a society viable.

The environment either supports a society's institutions, or it challenges and stresses them.

Sometimes environmental stresses have "natural" causes—drought, earthquake, floods, tsunamis, disease. Sometimes they stem from human causes. From inside—corruption, ethnic conflict, poverty. Or from outside—invasions, predators, epidemics, pandemics. Currently, because of drought, Niger and Mali on the southern edge of the Sahara can't provide enough food for their people. Societies in such marginal "natural" environments have a hard time sustaining themselves.

On the Front Lines of Instability

Afghan and Colombian societies can only sustain themselves by producing opium and cocaine. The environment offers them few alternatives; the institutions of government and the security forces are not capable of dealing with the problem; and the dysfunctional institutions that have grown up in these places—warlords and drug cartels—are difficult for the fragile positive institutions to cope with.

In Jordan, the institutions are reasonably sturdy. King Abdullah and the royal family have been responsive to the people and have been generally accepted by them, but the country is on the edge economically. There is no oil, water is hard to come by, and good land for farms is scarce. There are not a lot of environmental supports to work with.

Iraq has always had a positive environment—water, oil, an educated populace—but the country has never in its history had the right kinds of institutions. And its human environment, with three major conflicting divisions—Shia, Sunni, Kurds—greatly exacerbates all its other instabilities.

The Palestinian territories could be a functional society in terms of the ability to build their own institutions. The government is struggling to clean up corruption and achieve democracy; the people are educated and enterprising. But the environment in which Palestinians live has difficulty sustaining a functioning society.

Some of Somalia's neighbors—such as Yemen and Djibouti—are unstable, but they manage. They don't offer their people a wonderful life, but neither are their lives totally hopeless. The big questions: Can they sustain themselves? Can they get better? Or is the thread they're desperately holding on to going to break? In Yemen and Djibouti the institutions are barely hanging on; and it's very doubtful whether the environment can sustain a stable society. In societies that are so vulnerable, any pressures on their institutions, or any pressures on their environment, could cause them to collapse. What happens if the aquifers dry up or become saline? Or what happens if a tsunami hits and devastates? Are these societies resilient enough to handle stresses like these?

Some nations are unstable because of disruptive or dysfunctional systems that destroy or undermine stability. Such institutions override the positive institutions that should have been countering them. In Somalia, warlordism—a disruptive system—is the form of governance. That is the way the nation has ordered itself. In the nations that broke away from the former Soviet Union, the usual form of governance is authoritarian—another dysfunctional and disruptive system. Afghanistan has a very fragile federal system, but with strong local warlords. In Latin and South America, and in parts of eastern Europe and Russia, drug cartels and organized crime are virtually parallel governments—thugocracies. Iran is a theocracy; the clerics rule. Such institutions are not the viable and enduring systems that will keep their societies stable.

The rate of change—or even change itself—can contribute to instability.

For many societies an instability that people can live with outweighs the possible benefits of change. No one will deny that change is needed. But a too-fast rate of change can prove so disruptive that the society and its institutions will be overstressed. Instead of progress, change can generate disorder and chaos.

This is hard for Americans to understand. We don't like to wait: "Democracy is good. Your system of governance is bad. You have to go zero to sixty right now." We feel that we have the morally correct way to govern, to run an economic system, to run a society, to run a culture. We may be correct in these beliefs. I am convinced that we are. What we don't understand is that change can be very painful and unpredictable. Change has a cost, which we may not see.

On a recent visit to Saudi Arabia, I was chatting with a western educated, progressive friend who is also a very senior Saudi official who loves his country and deeply respects its traditions. "Look," he told me, "I value my wife as an equal. I want her to sit with me in the front seat of the car. I want her to be able to drive. I have no problem with that. But I can't do that right now. It's too destabilizing. It creates all sorts of disruptive problems and issues, many more than our society is able to handle. Our generation may not be able to move our nation that far that fast. The job of easing Saudi Arabia into women's equality may belong to the next generation, but it will happen."

Americans don't give a thought to women in the front seats of cars, or to women driving. But to Saudis, such things threaten their social order. Should they become more like us in this? I think so. But I also think they have the right to sufficient freedom to get there at a speed they can handle.

I had a similar conversation with Iranians pushing for change from inside Iran. "Most reformers call for patience," they told me. "We want to get rid of the clerics and the theocracy; but we reject a second revolution. We want change over time and within our constitutional process and without violence."

"Why are the bulk of the reformers so patient?" I asked them, like a typical American. "Why are you willing to tolerate this repressive regime that's slowly destroying a great nation?"

"We have already suffered through the pain, the violence, and the disruptions of our 1979 revolution," they answered. "One revolution in a lifetime is enough. No one who still has that memory in their gut wants to go through that again."

Americans don't normally understand patience. We don't understand that change is not simply a matter of short-term sacrifice, followed by an absolutely predictable outcome. Change is unpredictable. We don't know how it is going to come out. Change sometimes means paying a staggering price—a price Iranians paid in 1979 with tragically painful results.

We have not gone through that kind of instability or pain since our own Civil War. So it's difficult for us to grasp that the path we may be asking them to follow may be so painful, so unstable, and so unpredictable that people are reluctant to take it.

Even the process of creating democracy may be destabilizing and bring unpredictable consequences.

We demand of our friends: "Elections are good. Organize an election."

That's true, but not in every society. Without an educated electorate, without substantial and viable political parties, without a viable political and institutional structure to elect into, the act of holding an election is meaningless. If people are told how to vote at Friday prayers at the mosque and end up with a legitimately elected radical form of religious ideology, is that a genuine election?

THE RESTORATION OF ORDER

Order and stability return to failed, failing, or unstable states when their institutions regain sufficient strength to sustain them, and/or their environment can again protect and provide for them. Rebuilding institutions or the environment can come from within—people can raise themselves up by their bootstraps—or with help from outside.

The bootstrap approach can work, but success is rare. More likely, unstable or failed societies will self-order negatively.

Instability, disorder, and chaos are not natural states in human affairs. People will find ways to restore shape to a broken society. But they—and we—may not like the order they get, which often is imposed by opportunists seeking power or promoting an ideology. A few examples:

Somalia. Order returned to the collapsed nation in the form of feuding, warlord-led clans.

Afghanistan. In the 1980s, the Soviets attempted to impose their kind of order on Afghanistan. With our help, the Afghans threw the Soviets out. We then abandoned the Afghans to instability and disorder; and a new order emerged, imposed by the Taliban, the warlords, and Al Qaeda.

Haiti. In the 1990s, we launched a major intervention in Haiti (one of the world's twenty poorest states), and made Jean-Bertrand Aristide president. Later, when he proved to be corrupt and ineffective, the situation deteriorated once again. We resolved the initial conflict, but failed to resolve the postconflict. Conflict broke out again.

Iraq. No regime in recent times was more evil than Saddam Hussein's thugocracy. Yet, in the years after the first Gulf War, we effectively contained Saddam Hussein's regime. He was incapable of causing serious mischief outside his nation's borders. And though Iraq was far from a stable society, the instability was manageable. The cost of containment seemed far more acceptable than the cost of intervention.

Ignoring this reality, the United States and a handful of its allies forcibly evicted the Saddam Hussein regime, with no plans for a new order to replace it. Today, U.S. military forces in Iraq are mired in an ever-worsening insurgency. Civil war is an ever-growing danger. Disorder and chaos grow ever more entrenched.

The Islamic World. During the final decades of the Cold War, we missed the emerging turmoil in Islam—a historical event with political and religious consequences that will likely surpass those of the Protestant Reformation.

Islam—with over a billion people, a significant part of the world—has been hit hard by the onrush of modernity. Because the religious systems, political systems, and social systems in certain Islamic countries have not evolved to cope with it, adjusting to the change has been traumatic.

We have had many opportunities not only to see the turmoil coming but to recognize its myriad, intricate links across the Islamic world.

As early as 1979, Iran caught our attention in a big way—the fall of the Shah, the rise of the Islamist state, the taking of the embassy hostages. Yet once again, we were captured by the crisis and didn't see its part in the big picture: the emerging turmoil. We saw instead a small, isolated problem that we could handle tactically and operationally.

Now, in significant parts of the Islamic world, extremist movements have risen to become global threats. Nations that are vital to our interests—such as Saudi Arabia and Pakistan—are threatened. They are stable for now, but it wouldn't take much to tip them into instability.

The humanitarian, political, economic, and social problems of the Islamic geographical area, and the economic and strategic interests in energy, transport, and commerce encompassed there, have vastly magnified the disorder throughout the world.

South Asia. We are in the process of missing emerging turmoil in Central and South Asia, a vast and vital region that includes Indonesia, Thailand, the Philippines, Pakistan, Afghanistan, India, Iran, and the states carved out of the southern tier of the former Soviet Union. In this region exists a rich and complex mix of local and regional instabilities. If these grow worse, the consequences could be devastating. For starters, two South Asian states are nuclear armed; a third, Iran, is likely to be soon; and a major nuclear power, China, lives in the immediate neighborhood. Do we want to leave the region to find its own order?

With rare exceptions, standing back and doing nothing while nations or regions self-order is a program destined to create conditions that will come back and bite us.

Yet are we willing to take the steps necessary to create order and stability? Are we willing to accept the failure of the old models to address new realities? Are we willing to pay the price and make the sacrifice needed to fight instability?

We obviously can't declare war on instability.

We have already made the mistake of declaring war on one of its more dangerous symptoms—terrorism . . . and called it *officially* the "Global War on Terrorism." Think about it: We've declared war on a *tactic*—terrorism—*not* on an ideology, *not* on a nation-state. We measure success in this war *tactically:* in terrorists killed, finances disrupted, cells taken down.

This is no way to fight terrorism . . . or to fight instability.

Fighting an enemy *only* at the tactical level tells us we don't grasp the scope and complexity of what we're up against. Meanwhile, Al Qaeda is growing from an organization into a movement. Osama bin Laden's *strategic* and *operational* centers of gravity, his strengths at the *strategic* and *operational* levels—the continuous flow of angry young men willing to blow themselves up, for example, or his ability to preach as justification an unchallenged, aberrant form of Islam—go uninterrupted.

The same is true for our approaches to the other forms of instability.

We need a way to look at instability in all of its complexities, throughout its entire life span, in a holistic manner. We have to look at it from start to finish, with a comprehensive, integrated view that will provide the understanding needed to tackle instability before it metastasizes into a full-blown crisis with tentacles stretching all over the world.

At one time, the two worlds—the stable and the unstable—went their own ways. Now they cannot exist separate and distinct on this planet. And they are not just peacefully interacting. They are colliding. The collision does not manifest itself as a threat or a conflict in any conventional sense. Festering sores pass from their embryonic stages in the unstable world through a complex chain of events and eventually plague us in far different yet no less nasty forms. The chain between initial cause and final outcome is so long and often so obscure that we rarely understand the connection between the pain we end up feeling and the initial sore that sparked it. But the connection is there.

CHAINS OF INSTABILITIES

Every instability represents a real or potential human tragedy. But instabilities rarely come alone; they come as links in chains of destabilizing conditions. These chains may power conflict, disorder, war, and chaos that can touch all parts of the world.

The climaxes of that process—wars and crises—are big-time attention-grabbers. Rightly so. They announce loudly and dramatically that dangerous and violent events are underway, events that require serious attention and perhaps action from outside.

Most of us think of war and peace as opposites that get turned off and on by some kind of big switch: either peace or war. On December 6, 1941, we were "at peace." And then on December 8, we were "at war." Or, on September 10, 2001, we were "at peace." And then on September 12, we were suddenly swept up in a "Global War on Terror."

We define events by the crisis points. And then we deal with the crisis as though it's the only reality that counts. We lose sight of or fail to observe the chain of events and conditions that gave birth to the crisis. And then, once the crisis has been "fixed," we tend to lose sight of the chain of actions we must take to "recover" stability and achieve a workable end state (at least a condition of manageable stability) . . . or, beyond that, to "reconstruct" and "transform." As a result, the crisis may repeat.

The United States has long followed the "only crisis matters" model. We address worrying conditions in the world only when they have erupted into a crisis—that is, at the moment of greatest complexity and intensity along the chain of instabilities, the moment when taking effective action will be most costly and most difficult to resolve. For all kinds of reasons, dangerous developing situations don't catch our attention.

The early warning signs of famine are well known. International organizations monitor them and announce a developing hunger crisis. Yet, normally little attention is given to the growing hunger—in, say, Niger, Somalia, or Ethiopia—until the famine crisis actually hits and people are dying in the thousands.

How much better—and how much less costly—would it be if attention and effective action had been applied earlier in the process, when the crisis might have been prevented, and before the harrowing images started to hit the media or a direct threat to our interests drove us to act? We treat developing conflicts the same way. We ignore ethnic cleansing until we see genocide.

We have to look more closely at the chains and not just at their ends.

At one end: peace, stability, functioning systems, solid societies.

On the other end: conflict, confusion, chaos, crisis, fragile or failed societies.

In between, levels of destabilizing conditions which can grow and fester into conflicts and crises:

- Political. Ineffective governance and the inability to provide services and infrastructure you'd expect from a stable government. Government corruption; voiceless civil society.
- Security. Little personal protection. No effective police. Insufficient border security and porous borders.
- Environment. Poor agriculture management, pollution, overuse, and depletion of resources, rain forests, and water.
- Disease. AIDS, malaria, tuberculosis, and illnesses caused by unsanitary conditions and malnutrition.

- Natural disasters. Earthquakes and floods and the inability to deal with their aftermath.
- Nonstate entities. Drug cartels and other criminal enterprises are more powerful because the states are unable to cope with them.
- Demographics. Unchecked population growth.
- Longstanding ethnic and religious strife.
- Competition for limited resources.
- Migrations and refugees.
- Failed economies with massive unemployment.

These conditions don't exist individually and separately, but are twisted and tangled together. In parts of Africa, for example, poverty, drought, famine, AIDS, corruption, ethnic strife, and ineffective infrastructure are all mixed. This witches' brew of destabilizing conditions is not only a likely precursor of conflict, it drives the creation of chaos that threatens to wash up anywhere in the world . . . *even in the United States.*

THE LIFE SPAN OF INSTABILITY

When instabilities are left to grow and fester unchecked, bad situations worsen until they eventually explode into a full-blown collapse of order. That is what I mean by a crisis.

Crises take many forms. Emerging conflicts can turn violent and explode into wars. Failures to prevent the spread of diseases like SARS, TB, or AIDS can explode into regional or worldwide epidemics. Failure to manage water and land can explode into droughts and famine. Building mud-brick houses in earthquake-prone areas can lead to enormous loss of life and property damage when earthquakes strike. Failure to put in warning systems, as we witnessed in the tsunami crisis of December 2004, can lead to widespread catastrophe. And this, in turn, can destabilize a nation or society already on the edge, and perhaps push it into conflict and violence. Crises brew in petri dishes brimming over with unattended destabilizing conditions.

The Three Stages of Instability

I have pointed out many levels of these destabilizing conditions between peace and conflict—confusion, chaos, and war. We can look at these levels as stages in a larger system that describes the entire life span of instability.

We might describe these stages as an arc, moving from stability through intensifying instability and crisis and back down through recovery and, we hope, to a more manageable state (though without outside intervention and help, that stage usually remains unstable and the process will probably repeat itself).

We can map out on the arc the levels of instability:

The Simmering Stage. In the first stage, instabilities in a society will simmer. There will be a low level of chronic instability. The instability is a problem, but the problem is manageable. There will be holes in the society's institutions. There may be conflicts that look increasingly hard to resolve. At this stage the society is vulnerable to hits from inside or outside, or from the environment. As the simmering grows closer to a boil, the society grows increasingly vulnerable.

As conditions grow worse and the society rises higher into this stage, the society will encounter ever more complex conditions of instability. Instabilities will increasingly fester and erupt into conflict or other signs of crisis—though they may still be manageable.

The Crisis Stage. Higher still, the instabilities and conflicts intensify. The simmering grows even more intense; the society becomes increasingly vulnerable; there is usually (though not always) increasing violence. If nothing is done to stop it, it will begin to erupt into a crisis, violent conflict, or war. As the situation moves farther into the crisis stage, the society is likely to encounter much more widespread violence and the breakdown of order.

The Recovery Stage. No crisis lasts forever; it eventually winds down and gets resolved . . . or at least generates a state of exhaustion in which no one has energy enough or resources enough to maintain the crisis state. A violent conflict will find a resolution either through the victory of one side, general exhaustion, or a peace process. Famines or plagues resolve either when everyone who is vulnerable has died or when sufficient outside help arrives to feed the hungry or cure the ill. The society will make an effort to put itself back together.

During this stage conditions in the society can branch off in three directions.

First, the society might return to the status quo ante—a simmering state. That is, the crisis may reach a resolution but without the creation of stability.

Second, conditions may repeat—from simmering to crisis to simmering to crisis—sometimes again and again and again. We've seen this happen, for example, in Haiti and Somalia.

Those who have struggled, fought, or suffered through the crisis will rarely have available the capacities to correct the instabilities that gave birth to the crisis; and the society will have an even harder time recovering to a more manageable state. It will lack both the institutional and the environmental supports necessary. Unless efforts are made to correct the underlying instabilities, they are likely to fester again and reignite the crisis. The crisis will then come back with a vengeance. Afghanistan once again may be experiencing a failing recovery. All the states that previously made up the Soviet Union continue to work through a very rough passage into the new global environment. We thought we had resolved the crisis in Iraq by removing the Saddam Hussein regime. But that only popped the lid that had suppressed hundreds of underlying instabilities.

Third, the society may recover enough to start rebuilding and achieve true transformation (such as in Germany and Japan after World War II). A nation that has passed through a crisis may achieve a state of true recovery, reconstruction, stability, and peace, and even transform into an enduring stable state.

Such recoveries rarely occur without outside help from the United Nations, regional organizations, other nations, or NGOs, usually accompanied by some kind of outside military involvement to maintain security. (The military may also be called upon to take other roles and missions.)

Each of these stages presents outsiders with options for action. Action in the Simmering Stage focuses on preventing crisis. So for outsiders, the Simmering Stage becomes the Prevention Stage. Action taken during a crisis is normally an intervention to stop the crisis. This becomes the Intervention Stage. And on the downward, post-crisis slope, the Recovery Stage becomes, we hope, recovery assistance (which may only return the society to the precrisis status) or even transformation to full stability—the Recovery Assistance Stage. In that stage, outside efforts will focus on bringing the society up to a state of order and stability—or, failing that, at least to a manageable state.

The Prevention Stage. A simple truth, often ignored: Crises are easier to prevent before they erupt than to stop once they have erupted. The aim of the Prevention Stage is to stop collapse before a collapse occurs . . . and since collapse is almost always accompanied by conflict, to stop conflicts before they become violent . . . or to shape them in such a way that the damage is minimized. We try to mitigate the environmental stresses and to bolster, reinforce, or if necessary create institutions that will stand up to the shocks, disorders, and instabilities that threaten the society.

Once we have decided that an unstable situation needs attention, we then make an assessment of the situation on the ground—grievances, adversaries, history, root causes, and other relevant issues. A large part of the assessment process will focus on questions about levels of complexity. What's the security situation? Will we be facing humanitarian issues? (Answer: *very likely.*) And will the situation be complex, a mixture of issues? (Answer: *very likely.*)

Somalia was the most complex problem I dealt with. It had *every* problem.

Other, more simple problems are open to more simple solutions, as in the case of CENTCOM's small-scale humanitarian operation in Kenya (called Noble Response). We air-delivered food to several hundred thousand people who'd been cut off by floods. Our little operation saved 300,000 lives at the cost of $800,000. Though the Pentagon questioned the mission and tried to stop us from spending the money, we pushed back, forced the issue, and got what we needed. And we did immeasurable good. Had we waited until there was a humanitarian disaster, we would have had a far more difficult situation to deal with. And what might have resulted from that? Might Kenya have been partially destabilized? Would there have been a catastrophic humanitarian disaster that would have cost us more to resolve?

Once we have defined the problem, we look at how to prevent it. We have many tools available for action on the ground.

We start by looking at what is possible. Is negotiation the best approach? Capacity building—that is, institution building? Should we attempt an intervention of some kind? Do we try other incentives? A number of organizations can move in and engage in a benign way. Negotiation isn't the only possible action.

Next, we assess our own capabilities and the capabilities of everyone else involved. If we're in Somalia, we ask what can the Somalis do for themselves? How can we help them do more for themselves? Can we bring in regional organizations, like the East African Community or the African Union, who might be able to offer assistance or might help with some support from us?

Part of the assessment process will involve dialogue with all the parties involved to bring issues to the surface. We have to ask hard questions; we have to pose the problems. We have to judge the level of consent to a resolution of the problem. Do they consent to our involvement?

In Iraq, it's clear that there is not universal consent to our presence. Neither were the Somalis eager to have us—and they hated the UN.

We continue with further questions:

What can we offer? Arbitration? Mitigation? Compensation? Incentives?

In the case of conflict, can we contain it? With sanctions? With controls? With an increased military presence?

Can we engage? Can we help the people in conflict help themselves? Can we help them build capacities that will help them deal with the problems or crises? Can we change hearts and minds and help shape the environment?

Capacity building is key to constructing self-sustaining, stable societies. *Capacity*—broadly speaking—includes all the structures and functions of a working society: clean water, electricity, health care, education, a banking and finance system, a free press, police, justice, good governance, etc. We build capacities—like legal structures, economic development, political reform, but also health, education, environment, security—to reduce the forces of instability. Efforts to build capacities will focus on major institutions: political, economic, security, social and cultural, and humanitarian.

Political. The structures and rules laid down to manage and govern the various interactions in a society: the legal system, the decision-making system, the system for choosing leaders and decision makers.

Economic. The system for managing trade, occupations, money, finance, banking, and economic well-being.

Security. The system for providing order and public safety—for developing, controlling, and maintaining it.

Social and Cultural. The systems that govern and determine social interactions, faith, and traditions, and provide values. These systems give a society its foundation beliefs, and they frame a society's approach to such questions as: How do we deal with modernity? How will the fast-changing world affect our beliefs? How will we deal with human rights, human values, and the role of women?

Humanitarian. The health system, and the systems related to the people's physical well-being.

All these capacities interact: Security must be linked with rule of law. Rule of law always comes in a political context and usually is deeply rooted in the social structures. The health system can't function without security. Because none of these institutions stands alone, any attempt to go in with a single tool to take care of a single dimension—say, a military intervention to take care of security—is going to fail.

Similarly, if an area doesn't have enough water to support its population, we'll have to go in and look at their entire system—agricultural practices, industrial practices, waste, pollution. A solution might include acceptance of commercialization—that is, people have to pay for water (as most of us do). In some cultures, paying for water is seen as immoral; people have a hard time accepting it. A solution will certainly include water management—better purification, managing aquifers, building better distribution systems.

This kind of capacity building is good in itself. But it may also head off worse problems or conflicts, or help resolve a conflict that has already manifested itself. In parts of the world, water can cause wars over water rights, upstream usage and control, and the like. Rivers usually cross several countries. If the people upstream put up dams, the people downstream may not eat.

Or, we can look at other destabilizing conditions. Let's say we want to counter the radical Islamists who use madrassas to proselytize and brainwash children with hate, lies, and an education in religious studies that prepares the kids for the fourteenth and not the twenty-first century. USAID might fund educational programs that will not only teach reading, writing, and arithmetic but will provide a counterbalance and a more expanded education.

Or we can look at Afghanistan. One destabilizing factor in Afghanistan is warlordism. The country has been prone to warlordism throughout its history. To counter this we need to build up President Karzai's authority and make sure it's preeminent.

What does Karzai need to ensure that he's more than the mayor of Kabul, and can be effective everywhere in the country? He needs trained security forces that warlords don't want to take on—a national army, a solid police force. To accomplish that, he may further need to convince the local police in this or that town that he can provide for them from Kabul, and that they no longer have to depend on the local warlord. In other words, he needs the resources that will allow him to build schools and clinics; and he needs to be able to hold elections to set up the framework for proper government.

What can we do to help him in all these respects? We can train the military. We can provide economic support and investment. We can make sure Karzai has sufficient resources to reach out and start projects in the name of the central government.

None of these Prevention Stage actions is easy. The problems are always large and messy. And the question we will always have to answer: Is the effort worth it?

The Intervention Stage.   We have available several options for resolving a crisis.

In the case of a crisis that has erupted into a violent conflict, we can let the conflict run its course. We can let one side win or even help them win. We can try to persuade the contending parties to negotiate. We can try various kinds of military or nonmilitary interventions. Or we might use a combination of approaches.

Shooting, killing, and the destruction of homes, workplaces, and the other pieces of the primary infrastructure of living create a momentum that's hard to stop. Passions run high. Compromise seems a waste. The other side is evil, hateful, and treacherous. And though the costs of fighting are terrible, the gains seem worth it.

At times nothing less than a massive military intervention will put the lid on a conflict. And even then, attention must be paid to other tools for resolving the conflict, or else the war will likely resume once the military lid is removed.

The alternative to massive military intervention will often be to let the two sides duke it out until one or both of them are exhausted. This may seem cruel, but it may also be the only rational choice.

Resolution of the conflict often requires "ripeness"—a degree of consent that allows a resolution to be attempted, either through negotiations or through military operations.

The Iraqis wanted Saddam gone, but not under the conditions we were imposing on them. There wasn't a ripeness—a willingness to cooperate with our solution. Our method of resolving the conflict in Iraq was not only not ripe to the Iraqi people, it was not ripe to the rest of the world and to our allies.

Negotiations become an option when two sides reach a stalemate and both are at or near exhaustion. If one side is winning, or near winning, there's no negotiation. It's a dictation of terms.

Resolving crises requires integrating all the elements of power—diplomacy, information, military, economic, and even NGOs. Trying to solve everything with the biggest hammer—the military—is lopsided.

The Recovery Assistance Stage. After the society has resolved the crisis, the focus is on recovery. The initial aim is to build *at minimum* a condition of instability that is manageable (reaching the status quo ante is sometimes the best that we can do). Because conditions in countries coming out of violent conflict are always messy, and the desire for peace among the people is always uncertain, it's very easy to fall back into conflict.

The larger aim, however, is to take the situation beyond minimal recovery and to reconstruct the country's wounded society to achieve lowered levels of instability. Eventually—with resources, effort, wisdom, and time—it may be possible to transform an unstable society into a state of enduring peace and stability.

In the Recovery Assistance Stage, the tools, actions, and approaches are very similar to those used in the Prevention Stage—institution building, bolstering the environment, negotiation, mediation, security. But in this stage, the destabilizing conditions that originally produced the crisis have to be dealt with *along with* any destabilizing conditions produced by the crisis itself. Failure to organize a genuine recovery results in conditions like those we are now experiencing in Iraq.

The UNITAF/UNOSOM intervention in Somalia in the 1990s offers a powerful example of how following the approach I've described could have produced a better outcome. For starters, no investment was made in prevention or in early commitment, when minimal efforts would likely have prevented the violent and complete breakdown of that society. The knee-jerk intervention when the crisis hit came too little and too late. The recovery effort was disjointed and badly thought out. The consequences of these failures are clear to all of us who witnessed the catastrophic events unfold.

♫

The two worlds—the stable and the unstable—are colliding.

What do we do about it? What's the way forward for America?

I have described the arc of action—from understanding the conditions actually existing out there, through a goal-setting strategic vision back home, to actions that shape and manage the threats and challenges out there. But getting to the vision, and from vision to actions, is not as easy as it might seem. Not only do we face obstacles in the larger world, we face obstacles in our own government.

CHAPTER SIX

STOVEPIPES

Bureaucracy is the death of all sound work.
—Albert Einstein, 1934

Our nation's confusion about our role in the world is magnified by our failure to organize ourselves appropriately to achieve our goals there. There is a disconnect between the foxhole and government systems. Part of the disconnect stems from the obsolete way our government is set up to respond to world events.

The United States government is organized along functional lines. At the top of the structure are the executive, legislative, and judicial branches, each with its proper functions. The executive branch operates through functional departments—Defense, State, Justice, Commerce, Homeland Security, and so on—with various agencies—like FEMA or the FBI—operating functionally under the various departments. It's all very logical.

This organization very closely resembles the old military organizational model called the Napoleonic structure—because it was Napoleon's idea—and it was brilliant for its time. To some extent, the military is still organized that way.

This structure broke down the organization and staff along functional lines—administration, operations, planning, communications, intelligence, logistics, and so on. Each area operated on its own. Each was completely independent. Each pursued its function and no other. Each had its own heavily layered hierarchical command structure that processed only the information in its own functional area. The view of military operations from each function was very narrow—only what was in its own chain—and its view was not shared outside its chain. When it was passed on, it went up to the top, and then to the commander.

We call these kinds of narrow, top-down organizations "stovepipes."

It was a superb organization for the general on horseback who overlooked the field of battle from some high point while events played out below. The different functional leaders from time to time rode up to him and made their reports, and in his genius he gathered up their information, synthesized it, and made timely decisions.

Another example of our stovepipe system was our organization of separate military services. It gave us the foundation of great traditions and pride and the superb development of service skills. Yet, problems in building a joint war-fighting capability and battlefield synergy, in which all the military services would fight as one, were left to the highest level of national command to sort out.

This kind of vertical command or management structure no longer works effectively. The Napoleonic staff structure is too ponderous, too slow, too isolated, too layered. The battlefield today is far too complex and fast moving for such an uncoordinated and segmented system to provide useful and timely advice and recommendations to our leaders. The commander simply can't comprehend or synthesize all the information needed to describe the battlefield environment—and certainly not at today's tempos of operations (tempo being the ability to conduct relevant actions faster than your opponent). If he even tries, he's soon lost. And his decision process grinds away with no connection to actions in the field.

The synthesis has to happen earlier. We learned in the military that we can't just integrate the functions—intelligence, operations, planning—at the top. They have to be integrated at every level. Intelligence, for example, has to start talking to operations not through the commander but at every organizational level, and then the shared synthesis has to continue to develop through all the levels up to the commander, who can process the total synthesis from all components of the organization.

Our military made the change from a Napoleonic structure to the more flattened and integrated structure that we effectively use today. But the change didn't come easy. We fought it long and hard when it was launched twenty years ago with the revolutionary Goldwater-Nichols Department of Defense Reorganization Act. Militaries resist revolutionary changes.

Big changes come to the military and governments only after a major defeat, or when enlightened leadership forces a revolutionary move. In 1947, Harry Truman realized that the government's stovepiped military, intelligence, and foreign policy organizations were not functioning well—and he was wise enough to see that if the only person who could pull all these functions together was the president, then at some point the system was going to run up against a big crunch. So he pushed the National Security Act through Congress. The act created the National Security Council and the Joint Chiefs of Staff, which were to serve integrating functions at the top, as well as the Central Intelligence Agency.

The Truman revolution held until our nation's first major military defeat, in Vietnam, which pointed up the necessity for a more far-reaching revolution in military organization. The arrangement that Truman had created no longer proved effective; it didn't address the environment that existed.

In 1986, the Goldwater-Nichols act took the reorganization process much farther by forcing integration of the services. The military fought the legislation with every weapon of influence in their arsenal. None of the services wanted to lose their stovepipes. But a bipartisan majority in Congress passed the legislation which led to the functional integration that all our services actually embrace today.

Though the act has not achieved all its aims, we in the military have moved a long way in the right direction. We can clearly see the path.

In a stovepiped organization, the functional components at each level—A, B, C, D—do not relate to each other. They relate to their functional siblings on the other levels up and down the organizational system—As to As, Bs to Bs, Cs to Cs, Ds to Ds. In a more flattened organization, the functional components at each level are linked directly to each other. Representatives from B, C, and D join the A team. Representatives from A, C, and D join the B team, and so on. There is no separate and stovepiped integrating agency. Instead, each functional component becomes itself an integrating agency—an integrating team. Because all relevant components are represented on each team, all of them gain an ownership of each team and of what the team produces.

Thus, at the national level, each military service contributes members to the Joint Staff, which is the integrating team, and to its components. Similar integration happens at each relevant level of command below the national level.

Another stovepiped and dysfunctional bureaucracy, organized—like the pre–Goldwater-Nichols military—on functional lines, is the federal government itself, with all its stovepiped departments and agencies. Each of them—Defense, State, Intelligence, Justice, etc.—does its own thing. Each operates on its own. Each is independent of the others and pursues its own function and no other. Each has its own heavily layered, hierarchical command structure that processes only the information in its own functional area—and each fights to avoid sharing its view or its power outside its command chain. The only integrator of all these functions is the president himself at the top of the chain . . . who already has a lot on his plate.

Like the military, the federal government fiercely resists radical change.

The 9/11 attacks in New York City and Washington were another major defeat for our country. The 9/11 Commission was created to analyze the causes of the attacks and the vulnerabilities that allowed the attacks to succeed. The commission recommended greater government integration—for example, that the FBI and the CIA should share intelligence.

The post 9/11 recommendations led to the creation of two more stovepiped bureaucracies—the Department of Homeland Security (DHS), whose function is to integrate all the government functions that relate to nonmilitary security; and the National Intelligence Directorate (NID), which is supposed to integrate all the functions of intelligence. Neither is likely to succeed. Homeland Security does not have the authority or power to compel the other departments to give up any power they already have. And the NID is not going to integrate intelligence; it is simply another bureaucracy sitting on top of all the other intelligence bureaucracies.

In the end, we can't integrate organizations by creating additional stand-alone organizations. The lesson to be learned from the military experience is that we can't achieve true integration by creating more stovepiped structures and bureaucracy. We must draw on the existing organizations to contribute and be represented in the new structure. They must feel a sense of commitment and ownership or the new structure will just be another layer of competing bureaucracy.

Stovepiping Strategy

In addition to reorganizing and integrating the military, the Goldwater-Nichols act requires the president of the United States during the early days of his administration to formally present a national security strategy that, in the words of the legislation, will be a "comprehensive description and discussion," and to update it with annual budget submissions. In a well functioning government, the national security strategy presents a vision of how the administration aims to act in the world—a vision offering practical guidelines, not dreams or hopes; a wide-angled vision that looks hard at every relevant situation—from events near foxholes to the effects of dysfunctional government systems on our nation's ability to achieve its goals. If stovepiped systems impede our nation's ability to act effectively, the national security strategy would take that problem into account and suggest remedies. Reforming our stovepiped systems requires a clear national strategic vision. Without a clear strategy, we are wearing blindfolds.

When the national security strategy eventually comes out (rarely during the early days of an administration), it is generally fine sounding and vague, with all kinds of inspiring goals backed by the very best and most humane principles and values. But you won't find a real national strategy with clearly articulated ends, ways, and means.

The national security strategy is then supposed to generate a series—or a cascading—of subordinate strategies and work plans (all called by different names). The secretary of state develops a State Department strategy for diplomacy and foreign policy. This goes to his regional functional departments, who write what are called performance plans. Every ambassador then writes a country plan which is very specific. At the Department of Defense, the secretary of defense produces a national defense strategy; the chairman of the Joint Chiefs produces a national military strategy derived from that; the chiefs of each service produce individual service strategies; and the combatant commanders of the Unified Command (previously called CINCS, Commander in Chief) produce regional strategies, the Joint Staff produces functional strategies and concepts, which are all very specific. The Department of Homeland Security and other government agencies also follow suit with their strategies and plans.

All of these plans tend to be written in isolation. None of them—from the national strategy at the top to the very specific plans down below—is well cross-coordinated, let alone integrated. They all get created on top and funnel down the government's stovepipes. And though there's lip service paid to integration, nothing really gets integrated. Defense does its thing. And it does it in its hierarchical way. State does its thing. Homeland Security does its thing. Justice. Intelligence. And all the rest. And nobody truly brings them together. Everybody's turf is jealously guarded. In consequence, the national security strategy gives practitioners and operational people very little substance that they can use.

When I was CINC of CENTCOM, from 1997 to 2000, our day-to-day strategy—what we then called the Theater Engagement Plan—was supposed to be a theater approach to implementing the Clinton national security strategy (as modified and specified by Defense Secretary Bill Cohen in his "shaping the environment" policy, whose aim was to use our power and influence to bring nations in our region to greater stability). As our staff went through the process of developing our plan, it seemed wise—*indeed, essential*—to integrate our efforts with the State Department and other government departments and agencies to bring to bear all the capabilities of the United States in a focused way to achieve the administration's goals.

Integration never truly happened. I never found a way to effectively join forces with the State Department to link their plans with mine. I had no way to get answers to questions like, What's the diplomatic component of our strategy? What's the economic component? How is aid going to be distributed?

And yet we tried!

Through my superb political adviser, my State Department liaison, Ambassador Larry Pope, I communicated with my counterparts at the State Department, the regional assistant secretaries, and the ambassadors of the countries I was responsible for in the field; and I found kindred souls there. They wanted to cooperate.

Before I submitted my Theater Engagement Plan to the Department of Defense, I tried to share it with the State Department and with the individual ambassadors. It was a chance to make sure we were all on the same page and to build the plan from the bottom up.

But the Joint Chiefs came down on my head like a ton of bricks: "You don't share your plan with them. You give it to us. And we'll send it over to them once we approve it at the top."

But since I was not in the Joint Chiefs' chain of command (combatant commanders work directly for the Secretary of Defense), we did it anyway. I sent my plans over to State and the ambassadors in my region.

Since the Joint Chiefs knew they couldn't tell me to go pound sand, they went over to State themselves and actually threatened the assistant secretaries I was dealing with: if they accepted my draft plan, the Joint Chiefs would cut them off from DOD information.

The turf wars and jealousies can get *that* petty.

In my era, even if the CINCs produced good strategies at their level (and I believe we did), with good ends and reasonable ways to achieve them, we still had no idea whether or not the administration and the Congress would come through with the means.

For example, troops must exercise to learn, develop, and perfect their skills. The military has facilities for large-scale service exercises in the United States. And we also conduct regular, large-scale exercises with coalition partners in the regions. U.S. Army, Marine Corps, Navy, and Air Force exercises in the states and in global regions are important . . . and they compete for resources with each other.

Every other year we conduct a joint exercise in Egypt called Bright Star, which is the largest military exercise in the world. In exercises like Bright Star, our troops come out from Fort Hood or Camp LeJeune to operate in a real-world foreign environment with coalition partners, and they exercise the actual war plans that they would use in a real war in the same region and climate. Meanwhile, these exercises enhance the capabilities of the coalition partners.

This is how the planning for Bright Star might spin out.

First, I would submit to the chairman of the Joint Chiefs my five-year plan for exercises (the chairman controls the exercises budget).

He would look at the plan and determine the level of resources he could provide. He might say: "We don't have the money for that many exercises. You'll have to cut back." Or he might say, "Great. Go ahead. I'll bless your five-year plan. We'll support it."

If the chairman supports our plan, we can move on to the next step.

I'd then go to the Egyptians: "Okay, we're all signed up," I'd tell them. "We've got approval for the whole thing." It must be understood that this stage is very important, because from this moment on, the planning and operational machinery is chugging away. Putting on the brakes at this stage is difficult.

At this point, a service chief might testify before a congressional committee that he can't fully train his troops due to competing commitments on time and resources. (His mission, by law, is to train, organize, and equip his service.)

The committee chairman asks, "Why? What's the problem?"

"One problem is that the CINCs are requiring the troops to go off on too many joint exercises. That's not giving the troops enough time for proper service training back home."

There's no one there to counter the chief's statements or offer the other side of the story. The committee cuts the joint exercises.

My exercises are cut. And I have to tell the Egyptians the bad news. (My exercises were cut by over one-third during my time as CINC.)

On a visit to CENTCOM headquarters in Tampa, a congressman asks if I have any issues. "What are your problems?" he asks, "How can I help?"

"Our exercises budget has been cut," I answer. "We've planned for major exercises. Our Allies have planned for them. The chairman approved them. And then Congress cut them. It's hard to run big programs like that when you can never be sure they'll actually come off."

"No, you don't get it," the congressman says. "The cuts are meant to be a good thing. They free up resources for exercises back home."

"That doesn't make sense," I say. "The troops are getting good practice in both places. But here, we're practicing the war plan we have to fight, in the environment where we have to fight it, with the allies we have to fight with."

"Oh well, wait a minute," the congressman says. "We didn't know that. We cut your exercises because the service chiefs were telling us they weren't getting the training they needed."

"Yes," I say. "That's right. Their job is to train, organize, and equip the troops. And they have a standard set of training, organizing, and equipping objectives. My job is to fight and to prepare the troops to fight. I have a standard set of objectives of how we're going to fight.

"Look, the service chiefs are well intentioned. But you need to see both sides of the question. If you're going to cut, you have to understand what you're cutting and how to balance it. You just heard one side."

"Okay," he says, "I hear you. We didn't understand that part of it."

The problem in this scenario is the stovepiped presentation of requirements and issues. The service chiefs testify separately from the combatant commanders. Issues that must have an integrated presentation cannot be accommodated by vertical structures that do not share integrating agencies or mechanisms.

It's impossible for a regional commander to bring a forward-looking strategic vision to life when he has to scrape money together from year to year, and when he has no idea if a program he's started will move forward . . . or take a congressional cut. The rug can get pulled out from under him even after the chairman of the Joint Chiefs has committed to a program.

The military still has stovepipes, even after the Goldwater-Nichols act. The Bright Star story provides only one example of problems that still have to be dealt with before we can achieve true integration. The military learned through the growing pains of Goldwater-Nichols and all the dragging of heels that accompanied it that integration was more than simple deconfliction (staying out of each others' way on the battlefield), or coordination (exchanging information and communication). True integration means the ability to blend the powerful capabilities each service brings to the battlefield in a way to achieve the maximum effectiveness and efficiency.

All government departments and agencies face the same problems internally, and more difficult problems as they try to coordinate across departments and agencies.

In 1998, CENTCOM was given Central Asia, a block of five largely Muslim countries that had once been part of the USSR—Kazakhstan, Uzbekistan, Turkmenistan, Kyrgyzstan, and Tajikistan. This was a challenging—and daunting—addition to our region. The Soviet Union had fragmented; the resulting pieces were fragile and unstable; and these five front-line states faced serious external threats from Al Qaeda and Islamist radicalism as well as their own internal problems.

Yet no one in government pulled together those in the Departments of Defense and State and in Central Intelligence, and on down the line, to ask: "What are our strategic interests in Central Asia? What do we need to look at? Are some of the nations in a state of manageable instability? Are some beginning to erupt into conflict and violence? How should we approach these instabilities? Should we try to help the countries in the manageable state stay that way? What should we do about the countries falling toward crisis? What resources should we put toward our efforts? How should they be distributed? How do we coordinate our efforts?"

There were many actions we could have taken to try to stabilize that region and keep it from moving into conflict or crisis. We didn't take them. We had neither a coherent strategy nor an integrated set of programs that flowed from that strategy.

Stovepiping Power

Our nation projects each of our instruments of power—economic, military, diplomacy, information, culture, intelligence, and all the others—out into the world through the mouths of stovepipes. Each instrument of power is developed in isolation by the agencies that control these functions.

The State Department—like most other government agencies—does not have a "field" capability; its stovepiped view of its functions has never called for one. Our military has an enormous field capability; we can quickly send and support troops anywhere in the world, and they can almost instantly go into action.

♊

A crisis erupts somewhere in the world.

The Joint Staff and military planners in Washington instantly respond, providing the regional combatant commander with all the elements he needs to handle the crisis. The combatant commander and his staff marshal and focus these elements; and standing field units—battalions, air squadrons, ships—move quickly to the scene. The military can deliver logistics and infrastructure to operate anywhere, even in the most austere environments.

By way of contrast, the State Department has very little it can put on the ground in a crisis. They have policymakers and planners in Washington; and they have staffs in embassies. But they have no deployable field capability. They have to struggle to put effective teams of doers on the ground to apply the instruments of power that they should know best how to wield. The State Department is now attempting to create such a capability; but it remains to be seen whether they will get the resources necessary to support one that is truly effective.

In Operation Iraqi Freedom, in 2003, the military was responsible for the security piece of the operation. They showed up with 135,000 troops. They ran up to Baghdad and took it in days.

Those responsible for the political and economic reconstruction tasks showed up with a small pickup team scraped together from Washington agencies and embassies. There was no coherence, no vetting of qualifications, no true experience and training, no effective planning, and no pre-organizational structure. They were just thrown into an ad hoc situation.

Here's the inconsistency: the military is going to take care of the security dimensions, but where's the political "battalion"? Where's the economic "squadron"? There is no standing, ready-to-move field capability that can handle the political, the economic, and the other dimensions.

What happens when we run into a crisis in Haiti, Somalia, Sudan, North Korea, or Iran? State and other government agencies dig into their staffs, pick a bunch of people, and kluge them together. There's no cohesion, no preparation, no deep knowledge of the situation, no integrated planning with the other operational units. On one side we have the highly developed, well-planned, well-thought-out, coherent capability that the military can field. And on the other side we have an ad hoc, thrown together, disjointed, dysfunctional group sent out to wrestle with a giant mess of a crisis. When we toss that out in the field, we automatically fall behind the power curve in our critical ability to build or rebuild capacities in the political, economic, social, informational, judicial, and other dimensions.

The result: The security situation stagnates and deteriorates, because the rest of the team, no matter how well intentioned, can't do what they are supposed to do, and the military can't hold it all together. We can freeze the situation in place to give the others time to do their thing, but they have to be able to move their areas of responsibility forward quickly, or we lose the critical momentum gained in the immediate aftermath of military intervention.

Something ought to tell us: "We've got this formidable security capability in Iraq. And now we're trying to rebuild the country, at the make-or-break-point of our efforts there—where we're now launching social, economic, and political reconstruction. What we need in order to do that job is something akin to the military model."

Our nation must aim to provide the same discipline and resources for the organizations that deal with the problems of instability, disorder, and conflict as we provide to the military to deal with the problems of security—the same kind of planning, assessment, training, doctrine, organization, and education. We need to be able to field an equivalent deployable structure—trained, organized, equipped. And this structure and the military structure must be integrated in a larger operational and strategic structure.

It is not only a matter of revamping and replacing bloated, stovepiped government bureaucracies with more integrated, efficient structures. We must also be serious about reforming a system that condones pork projects that waste resources and a system of patronage that places poorly qualified cronies in critical positions of leadership. We can no longer afford these outdated and ineffective practices that adversely affect our ability to cope with this new complex world.

At the same time, we must overhaul our methods of dealing with instabilities and crises in the world, to move to closely match the world's complexity. Contemporary world problems are interconnected; they reach into the fabric of societies. They require carefully crafted and delicately balanced approaches to resolve them, approaches that must have both well-integrated contributions from and the active support of many sectors of our government. To be more comprehensive and effective, our new approaches to instabilities and crises must also incorporate international cooperation and the support of regional institutions.

Military responses by themselves will not do the job. We need to determine where we as a nation want to go, and we need to decide how we will get there. We need a new strategic vision for our country—a vision that will focus our government and all its elements of power on the task of bringing peace and stability to the world.

(previous page) Briefing President Clinton and other officials on a strike on Iraq

(left) In Vietnam as an advisor to the Vietnamese marines

(right) With Kurdish children in Northern Iraq

(below) Greeting a first responder from Central Asia during a CENTCOM exercise on cooperative disaster relief

Taking command of UN troops in Somalia covering the withdrawal of UN forces known as Operation United Shield

Speaking with Ali Abdullah Saleh, President of Yemen, regarding support for his border security and coast guard requirements

Meeting with Sultan Qaboos, ruler of Oman, at his desert camp

Shaking hands with President of the Palestinian Authority Yassir Arafat

Greeting Israeli Prime Minister Ariel Sharon

Discussions with King Hussein of Jordan about military aid for Jordanian forces

(above) On the site of a suicide bombing with Israeli President Moshe Katsav

(left) Meeting with Crown Prince Sultan, Minister of Defense of Saudi Arabia

Talking with Foreign Minister Abdullah Abdullah of Afghanistan on the future of his country

Reviewing Kyber Rifles at the Kyber Pass in Pakistan

(next page) Greeting President Pervez Musharraf of Pakistan

CHAPTER SEVEN

STRATEGY

Strategy—The art and science of developing and using political, economic, informational, and military forces as necessary during peace and war to afford the maximum support to policies, in order to increase the probabilities and favorable consequences of victory and to lessen the chance of defeat.

—Department of Defense Dictionary, 2001

We need to clearly understand where we're going as a nation, what we are trying to do, and what we want to be in ten years, or twenty-five years. These are strategic questions, questions of national purpose and direction.

A national strategy defines how a nation chooses to engage with the world. There are two ways to look at it. We can decide on our strategy and then use our power and influence to shape the environment to fit our strategy. Or we can take a hard, cold look at the environment to see how we can shape our strategy to achieve the best possible goals within the limits of the environment and of our power and influence.

The first option presupposes that we can totally control the environment. If we can do that, then we can state our strategy and shape the environment to fit it. The national strategy of Nazi Germany was based on the presumption that German power could dominate the environment.

If we decide we can't control the environment, then we have to be willing to put enormous energy and resources into understanding the environment and the threats the environment can throw at us. Here it's vital to learn from people on the front lines who see and experience the actual conditions existing in the world environment. Once we have achieved that understanding, we can build our purpose within that perspective. We have to understand our own power, our own capabilities, our own limitations. We have to understand the threats we can deal with, the threats we can't deal with, the opportunities that offer themselves, and where we have to make choices. We also have to understand how to build international cooperation and support to gain additional legitimacy and share the burdens.

As the wise Chinese philosopher Sun Tzu put it twenty-four centuries ago: "If you know the enemy and know yourself, you need not fear the result of a hundred battles. If you know yourself but not the enemy, for every victory gained you will also suffer a defeat. If you know neither the enemy nor yourself, you will succumb in every battle."

The United States is the dominant nation on the planet, but not omnipotent. We can't totally shape the world to fit our strategic vision. We're not that powerful. Our strategy has to take into account our own limitations and the limitations imposed by the environment—including the reality that there is no shortage of other international actors, from nation-states to terrorist groups, who will use every means in their toolkit to counter or undermine American policies.

Yet, we can greatly influence the environment; and we haven't realized our full potential in achieving that.

A strategy answers three questions: Where do we go? How do we get there? How much will it cost? . . . Ends, ways, and means (resources). It's an action statement and not, as some might think, rarefied ideas produced by rarefied intellects.

A national security strategy is the overall statement of those ends a nation wants to achieve and the ways and means available to achieve them. It is the overall description or vision of the conditions that exist out in the world, of how best to respond to those conditions, and why that response is necessary. The strategy provides the overall authority for the actions that follow from it and the overarching description of what all the component parts of government need to bring together in order to achieve the strategic aims. At its base must stand clear direction and consistent principles.

What *is* our national security strategy?

During the Cold War, America's strategy was well understood. Answering that question was easy: containment and deterrence of the Soviet Union. We were the bulwark and centerpiece not only in defending the world against communism, but also in helping the nations of the world gain their freedom . . . in terms of economics, governance, and social issues. The strategy was developed by George Marshall, George Kennan, and others. It was consistent. Everyone accepted it. It was transferred from president to president, from administration to administration. And it served well for nearly fifty years.

But a search for answers to that question today yields confusion.

Is our strategy anchored, for example, by humanitarian and human rights principles? The answer: sometimes yes; sometimes no.

If we send our military to intervene in other countries, the presumption is that the intervention is derived from our national strategy and its underlying principles and purposes, and from a clear threat to our articulated vital national interests.

Sometimes we have intervened in other countries for humanitarian reasons, as we did in northern Iraq and Somalia. But as we did not in Rwanda and Burundi or Congo or Sudan. We intervened in the Balkans for European security reasons; humanitarian considerations were not the controlling element in the choice. We went into Haiti because of the impact on us of illegal migration—not for humanitarian reasons. And if we were thinking pure humanitarianism, we would have gone instead into parts of Africa, where the humanitarian tragedy was far greater.

The inconsistencies don't stop there.

We have (somewhat timidly) intervened in Colombia in the hope of putting a check on the illegal drug trade. But until Al Qaeda forced us to move into action, we ignored Afghanistan, the world's largest producer of opium poppies. After the removal of the Taliban regime, poppy production soared.

Sometimes we have supported independence, as we did in East Timor, which is remote, half of a small island, with nothing like a sustainable economy. Yet it apparently deserved independence. On the other hand, the rebels in Aceh, in northern Sumatra, make what may be a better historical case for independence; and they have enough oil to support an independent economy. Yet we say that Aceh's problems have to be settled within the context of the Indonesian state. We have given a similar answer to the Kurds.

The current Bush administration has proclaimed a doctrine of unilateral preemptive intervention. Whether the Bush doctrine is wisdom or folly, it's undeniable that it has been applied inconsistently and haphazardly. Did Saddam Hussein really top the list of threats to the United States, or was North Korea or Iran more dangerous?

The process of answering questions such as these is what I mean by building a strategy: through the answers, we articulate our vision, set our goals, and determine the actions necessary to achieve our goals; we examine and allocate the resources available to us; we create the organizational structure and programs needed to implement our goals and track our progress.

Strategic Goals

We must set goals that will at least manage, or if possible heal, unstable conditions before they grow into crises; that will manage crises that do develop so as to reduce the unstable conditions that follow the resolution of the crises; and that will manage recovery in such a way that reconstruction or even true transformation will emerge.

Our nation's strategic goals should include:

- Keeping stable as many regions and countries as possible . . . and as we can afford;
- Moving countries into stability that are now unstable . . . where feasible;
- Building programs that counter destabilizing conditions;
- Investing in full recovery, reconciliation, and transformation in places that present the greatest threats;
- Building, with our support, regional capabilities to deal with unstable conditions;
- Outlining an international strategy that will encourage multilateral partnerships, contributions, and participation.

These principles are the basic underpinnings of any sensible national security strategy.

I am a pragmatist and a realist. Our nation can't do it all. We can't fix all problems. We don't have enough resources, money, energy, smarts, prescience, and attention to make the whole world stable.

But we can contain or deter the worst destabilizing conditions in places that are important to us. And we can bring back to reasonable positions of recovery places suffering through serious conflicts or crises; places that we aren't going to be able to fix, but that we can bring to a point where they'll muddle along and manage; places that we can monitor and ensure that they don't erupt into violence, crisis, or chaos.

This realistic and practical view of our national goals directs our attention to two critical needs: international cooperation and regional development.

We must create and support international and nongovernmental organization cooperation.

The United States can't go it alone. We cannot be out front on all emerging or breaking crises. Our national strategy will fail without close cooperation both with other nations and with international, regional, and nongovernmental organizations.

Though we have today a strained relationship with international organizations, it is clear that we need international cooperation to more effectively share burdens, gain legitimacy, and synchronize efforts. In our strategy, plans, and programs, we need to define what role we foresee and seek from international organizations (such as UN agencies), regional groups (such as NATO), allies, and nongovernmental organizations (such as charitable and humanitarian organizations). The growing consensus for reform of the United Nations offers an opportunity for cooperation with other UN members to create greater UN capabilities in this area.

We must, where appropriate, make the effort to persuade these organizations to create standing partnerships with us, to prevent the frictions we've encountered in ad hoc approaches. This does not mean that we will absorb their identity or tell them what to do. They must know that we are all working together toward goals we can all agree upon . . . and that we are not looking to dominate the process.

In cooperating multilaterally with others, we will not surrender our sovereignty or give up our own decision making. We're not inviting others to contribute to deciding our actions. Our national strategy is not an international collective decision.

After we make our own decisions and formulate our strategic policies, we can work out how to implement a strategy in ways that are cooperative and nonconfrontational, in a multilateral international context.

The recent South Asian tsunami crisis sparked an extensive commitment of NGOs and other humanitarian and disaster relief organizations from many nations and the UN. The magnitude of the tragedy made it essential that these disparate (and sometimes mutually antagonistic) organizations coordinate their plans, their programs, and their on-the-ground efforts. So far, the results have been positive.

We must create and support regional development.

We constantly agonize over commitments that stretch our resources and pull us into difficult situations that do not seem to directly affect our vital national interests. We lament the absence of local or regional capabilities to deal with the demands generated by crises.

In many cases, a small coherent investment in developing local capabilities within regional cooperative organizations would allow them to handle these problems . . . or, at least, handle them with minimal support from us. More importantly, this could be done with regional "boots on the ground"—and with support from us and the international community. In many cases, the local will is there, but the means and skills are lacking. Building and supporting these capabilities is an investment in stability and prevention.

I have been frustrated by our reluctance to recognize what could be accomplished—and what could be saved—by promoting and supporting such programs.

Because regional organizations do not automatically make up for the inability of nations to work together, cooperative mechanisms have to be created. When I was commander of CENTCOM, a major goal of Secretary Cohen's "shaping the environment" policy was to build the mechanisms that would develop the ability of nations to work together on their own . . . and more generally to build up their confidence and their capabilities in dealing with security issues. My regional strategy attempted to answer the question that followed directly from that charge: "What can CENTCOM do to build confidence, capacity, and cooperative mechanisms . . . and through that greater order and stability?"

The East African Community (EAC) is made up of three nations struggling to stabilize their region—Kenya, Uganda, Tanzania. They have a strong motive. Spillover from failed states and the resulting regional chaos has left nasty scars—especially in Kenya. With no Somali government to curb it, the lawlessness in Somalia washed down into northern Kenya. Bandit gangs ran raids; warlord militias made incursions; Somali clans and tribes crossed over into Kenyan territory looking for safe haven. The refugees had to be somehow cared for; law and order had to be somehow reestablished; and all the while, the refugees were fomenting Islamic fundamentalism in the heavily Muslim areas of Kenya along the coast and around Mombassa. Instability originating in Somalia spread through Kenya.

Building up their peacekeeping forces would provide the Kenyans and the other EAC members with the capability to take action to prevent the chaos next door from falling into their own backyard. But they were also willing to use their militaries in peacekeeping missions in other, more distant parts of Africa. The results of their interventions have not always been encouraging. In 1999, the Kenyans took part in a disastrous UN intervention in Sierra Leone, which was later salvaged by Canadian and other forces.

Kenya, Uganda, and Tanzania—the Kenyans especially—had solid militaries, but with the deficiencies in training and equipment we've come to expect in poor countries. However, properly provided with military training, equipment, transport, intelligence, and logistical support, as well as training in mediation, negotiation, and working within other countries—all of which we could easily do at low cost—they'd be ideal in the peacekeeping, humanitarian, and crisis-prevention mission.

I knew that an emerging crisis in Africa *might* catch the attention of the United States, and we *might* be motivated to take action against it . . . but never in the early stages when a crisis can more easily be fixed. I knew that America reacts only when a crisis has metastasized into a major catastrophe . . . after the media has started covering it and we see images of bomb-blasted villages, massacres, and starving women and children. And I knew it would take a strong dose of horror to generate in this country sufficient popular backing, congressional support, and funding to launch a humanitarian relief operation. But by then, the crisis would have already erupted, and it would be much more costly and difficult to resolve.

"Far better for Africans to take on this role," I thought, "especially if they can take the early actions Americans are reluctant to take. If we do this work well, we'll develop islands of stability that will 'infect' their neighbors and spread out like green in spring."

With all that in mind, we initiated a program to make good the EAC's deficiencies.

It immediately ran into an institutional roadblock. Kenya was in our CENTCOM AOR (Area of Operations); Tanzania and Uganda were in EUCOM's. We asked if the two countries could be moved to our AOR, but EUCOM objected. Though we then agreed to work the program jointly with EUCOM, the effort never really got going. Even so, we did make good progress in Kenya.

The program had three elements.

At the tactical level we already had a running program, called ACRI (African Crisis Response Initiative), aimed at training and equipping individuals and small units for humanitarian and peace-keeping missions. ACRI was a worthy effort, and it was successful— as far as it went—but it was too small scale to give the Africans the kinds of real-world capabilities they needed.

They needed help at the operational and strategic levels. Specifically, major exercises and field training at the battalion and staff levels. To that end, I took ACRI several steps higher by bringing together regional African and American forces in an annual brigade-size field exercise called Natural Fire. The exercise focused on a realistic humanitarian and peacekeeping task. The militaries worked alongside NGOs and international relief organizations; and our own medical, dental, and veterinary teams provided further training. (They actually did a lot of good in local villages.)

At the strategic and policy levels, we brought in senior military, political, and NGO leaders to discuss the joint decision-making process in humanitarian missions. Specifically, they sought to answer the question, How do we reach consensus on the big operational strategic decisions and bring the various elements together on the ground?

I had earlier experience starting programs like these. Back when I was a lieutenant general, commanding the 1st Marine Expeditionary Force (I MEF), we launched Emerald Express, a high-level forum for these very kinds of discussions which became the model for Golden Spear, which was solely focused on engagement issues in Africa. The first Golden Spear conference was held in Kenya in 2000.

Today, the African Union is willing to take on the Darfur crisis in Sudan, yet it is struggling to do so. Little has been done to build the capacities of the member nations to intervene and resolve such situations. Too often, African organizations have intervened and stumbled or failed in places like Liberia and Sierra Leone. It is in our own interest, and in the interest of other first-world nations, to build serious pre-crisis capabilities in these organizations and to support our commitment.

International cooperation and the development of regional institutions that can manage crises and assist other nations in the region must be an integral part of formulating our own national security strategy.

A clear and comprehensive national security strategy will answer the big questions about strategic vision—where we want to go, what we're trying to do, and why we want to do it. But it does much more than that. It drives the policies, programs, organizational structures, and resource allocations that bring the vision to reality.

A business is about to make a major sales presentation. In order to do that the CEO (or perhaps some deputy) will produce a vision of what he wants to accomplish and the means available to achieve it. He will look at the tools available to make the presentation come alive. He will look at the people best equipped to make the presentation. He will look at the audience he intends to sell to. And he will look at all the other factors that will influence the presentation. Every one of these factors flows directly from the vision. Take the vision away and the presentation becomes chaos.

A family is about to leave for vacation. Before they pile into the car, they will have a vision of where they are going and how they plan to get there. The vision is first of all based on their knowledge of the vacation spot. The vision then sets the goals and plans for the vacation, and once these are in place, the family can execute the vision. Take away the vision and the family piles into their car and sets off for wherever the wind blows them.

Strategy is not realized in ideas. It is realized in the foxhole. It must drive actions and the systems and structures that produce actions.

CHAPTER EIGHT

FROM STRATEGY TO FOXHOLES

As presently configured, the national security institutions of the U.S government are still the institutions constructed to win the Cold War. The United States confronts a very different world today. Instead of facing a few very dangerous adversaries, the United States confronts a number of less visible challenges that surpass the boundaries of traditional nation-states and call for quick, imaginative, and agile responses.
                                              —9/11 Commission Report, 2004

Pursuing a strategy aimed at building greater stability and order in the more unstable parts of the world will require government organizations and systems that can effectively reach that end. Since our archaic stovepiped governmental systems at best hinder and at worst obstruct the carrying out of any strategy, a new approach to structure would better integrate our governmental functions and capabilities at the national level and down to the implementation level. The 9/11 Commission and the congressional committees that examined the 9/11 failures clearly saw the problem caused by lack of integration, coordination, and cooperation in the areas of intelligence and securing our homeland. Unfortunately, the solution they offered—creating additional stand-alone bureaucracies—did not, in my view, solve the problems.

What follows is an approach to these reforms that I believe is more viable; it's been successful for the American military; and it can be easily adapted to other large organizations. But it is not the only possible path to reform.

Working from the strategy to the foxhole is like erecting a building. You begin with the architect and the design. That design is passed to the structural engineer, who must ensure the design is sound in every respect. He plans the detailed integration of all the parts involved in making the building functional and efficient. His plan is passed to the builder, who must oversee the actual onsite construction. He sees the problems on the ground and must make the design and structural plan work. All three—the architect, the structural engineer, and the builder—must work together in an iterative process. The parallel to this is the strategic, operational, and tactical levels of the military model. This model should be our framework for changes in our governmental structure to deal with the new set of problems we face.

FOUNDATION

My approach is based on the military's three-tiered strategic, operational, and tactical structure because it offers enormous efficiency and flexibility, and because the military already has generations of experience with it. My approach also adapts to our government the military's efforts to eliminate stovepipes by integrating and flattening organizations. No enterprise—business, government, nonprofit, international organization—can function effectively and efficiently in today's environment unless it is flattened and integrated to the maximum extent. Things move too fast. Competition is too tough. Decisions are too complex.

The military is the only governmental organization that fully develops and works in the strategic, operational, and tactical areas. At the strategic level, it already has the Department of Defense and the Joint Chiefs of Staff. At the operational level, it has regional unified commands—European Command, Southern Command, Pacific Command, and Central Command. At the tactical level, it has deployable squadrons, brigades, battalions, and ships. Any actions or interventions the United States is likely to undertake to bring order and stability will almost inevitably have a military component. The military also has retained its support structure (the military services that train, organize, and equip) and effectively blended it with the operational structure.

I know this framework well; it's deeply embedded in my thinking; and it works. And yet, even though our military took to it generations ago *because* it works so well, it is *not* an exclusively military way of thinking or of organizing actions. Every well-managed organization will have an executive to plan and shape larger goals, directions, and purposes. It will have a force on the ground to implement the goals and plans—in the shops, stores, factories, offices, or building sites. And in between, it will have a level of operations to translate the executive's plans and goals into a form the people on the ground—those in the foxholes—can use. In other words, strategy, operations, tactics.

Successful businesses continually seek to flatten and integrate their organizations. It is the most efficient, effective, and responsive way to accomplish their business goals, especially in high-tempo enterprises.

At the strategic level, structural changes in our government will result in an organization that will integrate the relevant national-level organizations, agencies, and departments, and using their expertise and inputs will continue to look closely at what's developing in the world, while building plans and programs for dealing with it. It will also recommend the application of our resources to achieve maximum effect and payoff.

Implementing these plans and programs will require coherent and integrated organizations at the operational (or regional) and tactical (or feet-on-the-ground) levels.

Since we already have an existing operational level structure that performs its role extremely well, and that matches up with the way any well-working organization will naturally operate—an executive to determine plans and goals, an integrating management, and a field force—we don't need to look for another kind of structure. Even if it made sense to create a new kind of somehow nonmilitary structure, we'd then have to adapt the already existing military structure to it, or else risk having one that doesn't match up with the military and that creates gaps in coverage.

The idea is not to "militarize" government, but to adapt to government a time-tested organizational approach that the military—among others—has used with great success, to draw on the lessons that the military learned through trial and error. The services did their best to resist the integrating reforms presented by the Goldwater-Nichols Act of 1986. We were forced to reform, but we improved because of the reform and the adaptive organizational changes that were made.

THE MILITARY MODEL

When the military stopped fighting Goldwater-Nichols and realized that integration of functions actually wins battles and saves American lives, we started to look hard at how best to do it. It hit us pretty quickly that the functional (though stovepiped) staff system—operations, logistics, planning, intelligence, communications, and so on—

was so ingrained and traditional that we couldn't simply disband it. That system was actually still useful in day-to-day nonoperational management. We still needed the functional organizations to perform their basic functions.

So we created a number of agencies, or cells, to integrate their functions from inside the functional organizations; we did not make these integrating agencies separate and distinct from the existing staff organizations. Each organization—like operations or planning—would be assigned a permanently staffed core, but all the other functional agencies would contribute staff to integrating cells within operations or planning so that they all participated in what was going on. They all had a vested interest in operations or planning and felt some sense of ownership.

In the old, pre–Goldwater-Nichols days, we would start with intelligence assessment and planning. Once the plans got made, we'd hand them over to operations. The operations process would then get passed on to the logisticians, who'd hand it over to the communicator, who'd then hand it over to the commander's staff, and so on. . . . The process simply got too slow and unwieldy. We had to bring the functions together.

At a present-day Operations Center in each command we now have a thin skeleton group to keep it running and take care of the daily operational decisions. The director of the Op Center (as it has come to be called outside the military) has a few people to make the systems work, operate the computers, and monitor and manage current operations. But in the Op Center he also has representatives from logistics, from communications, from planning, from intelligence, and from all the other staff components—each contributing their functional expertise to the day-to-day running of the Op Center.

The same thing is happening at the planning centers. All the functional areas have contributed to planning the next phase of the current operation. And all the functional areas have contributed to planning the next mission. Planning is integrated. The military has additionally been working on what is called "collaborative planning"—in which several vertical levels plan collectively rather than serially. This lessens the number of planning organizations, saves critical time, and ensures understanding of the planning and planning factors.

The same thing is happening at the center that's managing the movement of forces. A logistician is there, a transportation expert is there, operations and planning experts are there, an intelligence expert is there. Recent innovations have also capitalized on advances in information technology to allow for greater span of control—meaning command elements can now control a greater number of subordinate units because of improved ability to process and move information.

In the military we've begun to flatten the organization. All the components of the organization provide their functional expertise at each level of the organization. All contribute. All put in their two bits. All have a direct connection with what goes on inside each level; and information is shared horizontally and vertically and across functions. The "product" is jointly produced. Everybody owns it.

Besides this functional integration, we have successfully integrated the military services contributions to the joint structure. The services provide the manning of the joint organizations and service components to work within these organizations. Hence, the contribution, sense of ownership and participation, and confidence in representation is promoted and maintained.

That model has made the military system far more efficient, far more flexible, and far more responsive to all the components of the organization and to fast-moving changes and new challenges. We can now move at a far higher tempo than under the old system. Because we can process information much faster, deliver to commanders already integrated information, and operate more quickly than any other military, our system has become so powerful that we can quickly defeat other systems' decision processes.

By way of contrast, the old Soviet system was heavily layered and top-down . . . stovepiped. The Soviets weren't even equipped to take information from the bottom up: their tanks had no transmitters, only receivers. The Iraqi Army was organized according to the Soviet system. When we fought Iraqi military forces, they were invariably trying to think while we were already doing. And we were by then already thinking about our next two moves. They would set all their players up close to the line to prevent a short gain, and we would throw and complete a long bomb. We could think and plan in dimensions of time and space that their system could not compete with.

The new governmental integrating organizations that I propose will follow the model of our military. They will bring together all the government's resources, powers, and wisdom to the task of confronting the great international challenge of the twenty-first century—creating and building order and stability in unstable and chaotic parts of the world. These reforms will function at the strategic or national level, at the operational or regional level, and at the tactical or boots-on-the-ground level.

In creating these new organizations, we don't have to throw out the whole gigantic governmental structure and start fresh. That would be unrealistic. The Department of State, the Department of Defense, and the other government departments and agencies work well enough within their particular areas of competence. They don't fail at the functional level. Their failure is in their obsolete stovepiped structures that block effective communication and collective actions. My focus is on the integration of the existing agencies . . . without taking anything away from their existing power, contribution, or status.

The integrating organizations will not be separate stand-alone bureaucracies, like the Homeland Security Department, the National Intelligence Directorate, or the National Security Council. We can restructure government by creating integrating organizations to which all can contribute their knowledge, their expertise, and their power. We pull them all together through their contributions.

AT THE STRATEGIC LEVEL

At this level we should create in Washington an organization that draws on all the resources available from all government departments and agencies to give our national leadership a cohesive, integrated picture of what we face day-to-day—an integrating agency that develops and ensures integrated plans for dealing with problems. It can pull together the resources and authority to construct programs that help prevent crises, shape nations, and guide regions toward greater stability.

The proposed organization could be called the National Monitoring and Planning Center (NMPC). It would be responsible for monitoring unstable areas, destabilizing conditions, and emerging threats, regardless of their nature: conflict, environment, corruption, health . . . anything. Its job would be to watch for the beginnings, the signs of growing instability—mounting tensions, grievances, little sporadic acts.

The NMPC would be an *integrating* organization. It would not provide a single view, but all views. It would be a joint, intergovernmental team; every relevant agency would provide representation and input. Its uniqueness would be based on its cross-representative nature: There would be an intelligence capability; an operational monitoring capability; a planning capability. It would have ties with the Department of Defense, Joint Chiefs of Staff, the State Department, Homeland Security, Justice, OFDA (the Office of Foreign Disaster Assistance), EPA, and any other agency that could add to the team's capabilities.

For example, representatives from the many, separate intelligence agencies in the government would provide the NMPC with their agencies' views of the unstable parts of the world. The NMPC would take all of these separate perspectives into account and then integrate them; it would not have a separate, distinct view, or its own means of access to intelligence. From this integration would come the ability of the NMPC to monitor the situations of greatest concern. If Uzbekistan, Zimbabwe, or Venezuela showed growing signs of instability or conflict, the NMPC would provide the National Security Council (NSC) and the president with a comprehensive and multilayered view of actual conditions in each of those countries, drawing on other departmental and agency assessments and fusing them. Or if the president asks about current conditions in Darfur, the NMPC could provide an integrated view taken from the best intelligence sources.

The NMPC would be structured along the general lines of a military command center and a military integrated planning cell (with representatives from each element—operations, intelligence, planning, and so on). In addition to a small cadre of permanently assigned personnel, it would be primarily staffed with planners and other members drawn directly from the other government agencies, to ensure confidence that each agency has direct input and involvement.

It would report to the president and the members of the National Security Council (the so-called principals) and would not have directive authority, which would remain along the existing lines of authority. The director of this agency would not be a cabinet position.

Though it would be structured like a command center, it would not replace existing command centers such as the White

House Situation Room and its counterparts in the State Department, Pentagon, and elsewhere. The NMPC's plans and programs would not replace the normal planning functions of State, Defense, Intelligence, or any of the other agencies, but would simply integrate where integration is needed or fill in missing pieces or highlight and explain conflicting differences. The change would not be a radical transformation. Existing departments and programs would still be necessary.

Since State, Defense, and the Central Intelligence Agency will not always produce the same analysis or reach the same conclusions, the director of the NMPC would report on their differing perspectives. His staff would analyze and highlight the differences, showing how each organization arrived at its own particular analysis and conclusions. They would try to provide this integrating analysis in an even-handed way, without voicing an opinion for or against a particular view.

The integrated view would not ignore or play down friction points between departments and agencies. On the contrary, it would point them out so that they could be effectively addressed and so the members of the NSC could understand why different assessments existed from those developed by their own departments and agencies.

The NMPC would also be responsible for developing integrated plans and programs to build order and stability in countries or regions of concern during any of the phases of instability. These plans and programs would be based on the plans and recommendations from other agencies and from people in the operational regions or out in the field. It would build the elements necessary to integrate existing plans. It would not create the plans for, or replace the plans from, the departments and agencies. When necessary, it would advise on intervention, and would monitor all the dimensions of intervention, recovery, and reconstruction. As the plans and programs became operational, the NMPC would track their implementation.

As things are now, the State Department has what they call performance plans, or country plans. The Defense Department has their functional plans and war plans, and the regional commanders have their regional plans. These plans are currently poorly integrated with each other.

The Department of Defense has a war plan for Korea, for China, and for Iran. But these plans all start at some moment of crisis that will switch on a military response. The department has no plans aimed at preventing wars before a crisis arises. They don't consider programs to build order and stability in the prevention stage that can cool off a conflict before it lurches into violence or war. And once the military has ended the crisis, Defense has no plan for reconstruction. The State Department may have ideas about prevention and reconstruction, but these have no relation to the military's plans, nor can State provide much in the way of people on the ground to implement their plans.

The NMPC would integrate State's plans with Defense's plans, and with any other plans that might be relevant, and point out where the plans will be effective and where they have holes. The NMPC would also help review integrated programs submitted from the operational level to ensure national level support and coordination.

How Will It Work?

The NMPC team would gather the data, assess it, and make recommendations. They would not make decisions; they would simply advise: "Violence is building in Nigeria—with its oil, strategic location, and large multiethnic population. The country is showing signs of falling into violence and civil war."

The team would ask: "What is our strategy for dealing with that situation? And how does it get implemented? What programs do we have working in Nigeria and in the region? Do we need to strengthen them or implement others?"

They would report to the National Security Council and the president: "We have looked hard at the problem, and we see the following destabilizing components. . . ." They would then make recommendations whether to commit resources and which resources to commit. The president would make his decision based on these recommendations.

If the president decided that the problem in Nigeria required U.S. attention, the team would review existing plans and programs for implementation, or create contingency plans for emerging crises if no existing plans applied; and they would review the tools available for implementing the programs and pull the appropriate tools into the integrated program.

The "tools" are the component parts of the programs at the tactical level. The programs integrate the tools, creatively combining them in order to build capacity in an unstable society.

If the erupting conditions in Nigeria metastasized into conflict, the team would get beefed up into a Crisis Action Team (CAT) or a Battle Staff level of manning—the way the military beefs up Op Center staffs during crises or wartime. The NMPC would then expand into the Inter-Agency Crisis Management Center: The team knew the conflict was brewing; steps were taken to prevent it; prevention failed. . . . Or maybe the crisis hit out of the blue (as did the Indian Ocean tsunami). . . . So now they would shift seamlessly into the actions needed to manage the crisis. Meanwhile, they would start to plan for the next stage, the recovery. The lines of input from everybody needed to get that moving would already exist; they would have been working the problems; and now they would be ready to handle the recovery and reconstruction.

During the recovery stage, the team would integrate the elements of power—diplomacy, information, military, economic—in order to make sure the crisis did not reignite. They would also monitor progress well after the crisis had passed, to ensure implementation and to assess the success of the recovery.

It's like a military operation.

If somebody says to me, you have to cross a river over there, I know how to do river crossings. I have a doctrine for that (that is, a preexisting set of concepts, processes, and procedures); I know how to organize the special equipment I need; I know how to put together the resources and conduct the operation.

Similarly, the NMPC would select from the available tools, pull them together into a cohesive program, and train and exercise this capability. The team might have to develop a specific program for particular conditions. Sometimes they might be able to take already existing programs off the shelf. Or they might tailor existing programs. The programs might be focused either on location-specific problems—countries, nation states, regions—or chronic problems, like environment, drugs, terrorism, weapons proliferation, or organized crime.

Thus, NMPC might decide to build greater security capacity in the Middle East as one of the programs to help fight Islamist extremism. And that might mean it would need to create a cooperative security program. So it might work with regional security groups like the Gulf Cooperation Council (GCC) and help them build up their collective security capabilities. Or it might look at the Far East where there are areas of rising Muslim insurgencies, as in the southern Philippines. Maybe it would recommend more diplomacy, mediation, incentives, and local capacity building for the civil society.

When I was the commander of CENTCOM, one component of our engagement plan was to help Yemen (a poor, tribal country of shaky stability, strategically located at the major sea-lane crossroads between the Persian Gulf, Africa, and Europe) to build up their counterterrorism forces and border security. Yemen was the terrorists' open gate in and out of the Arabian peninsula—a long, empty coastline, no coast guard, no border security. Our aim at CENTCOM was to help them guard that gate.

One step on that path was to help Yemen build a coast guard. In order to make that happen, I had to go to multiple organizations— for example, to get Yemen on the list to receive what are called "excess defense articles" (say, boats the U.S. Coast Guard had declared obsolete) or to find spaces for Yemenis in the International Military Education and Training (IMET) program. Putting together a little coast guard for Yemen meant jumping through a massive array of stovepiped hoops back home to assemble the myriad pieces necessary to make the program viable. There was no cohesion—no cooperative or integrated way to look at such things or to build integrated programs.

The NMPC would do all that. They would work with the people at the operational and tactical levels, look hard at the situation in all its complexities out in the field and within our bureaucracies. They would draw together the different departments and components of what it would take to form a coast guard and to make it work. They would then build the necessary program and present it to the NSC for a decision about whether or not to make it happen.

In order to lessen instability in South America, NMPC would take off the shelf programs aimed at the region and at chronic problems there—such as drugs—tailoring them as necessary. It would also use country-specific programs, and programs aimed at specific destabilizing conditions, such as the FARC rebels in Columbia. A military component of this might involve increased training and equipment; the Justice Department might increase police training and law enforcement cooperation; the Agriculture Department might work with its counterparts to develop markets for alternative crops to cocoa; the State Department might work to develop regional cooperative programs and efforts.

This structure would eliminate the need to create so-called czars (such as the Drug Czar) for special programs that the president sees a need for. The NMPC would pick up responsibility for these efforts and expand them with support from appropriate agencies. These would provide special substaffs necessary to deal with an emerging serious problem or crisis.

Finally, the NMPC would coordinate and jointly plan with international and nongovernmental organizations, and help build partnerships with regional organizations, where appropriate.

AT THE OPERATIONAL LEVEL

Executing the NMPC's programs would take place at the level between Washington and the field. At this level all the elements are integrated—the plans and programs from above and the actions to implement them on the front lines below.

In the military this is called the operational—or regional—level. Both the State Department and our military unified commands—CENTCOM, EUCOM, PACOM, SOUTHCOM—are organized regionally (though the State Department's and the Pentagon's regions have different boundaries).

The military's regional unified commands represent the only truly viable organizations at the operational level that could plan and monitor the implementation of the programs developed or reviewed by the NMPC. But the military needs help. It could only execute the dimensions of the programs that lie within its own competence and its capabilities.

We would need a counterpart organization to deal with the political, economic, informational, social, humanitarian, and other dimensions of the issues we face, and to join with the military in implementing the NMPC's plans and programs.

Recently the military's Joint Forces Command and several regional commands have tested a complementary organization—called a Joint Inter-Agency Task Force (JIATF) or Joint Inter-Agency Coordination Group (JIACG)—co-located with the Unified Command Headquarters and staffed from the appropriate nonmilitary agencies: political, medical, economic, cultural, environmental, etc. In the exercises, experiments, and operational events, these organizations were stood up as temporary ad hoc staff adjuncts. They participated in planning and provided a civilian agency perspective on military operations; they provided links between the military and the civilian agencies; and they were involved in crisis planning and assessment.

These experiments have demonstrated the value of closely coordinated, multidimensional cooperation at the operational level; yet we obviously still have a long way to go before we can turn this very limited, very temporary, kluged together organization into a force that can balance and complement the very powerful, unified command staff that does military planning.

We should take this concept and organization to its logical end: the JIATF/CG and unified command combination should perform the equivalent function at the operational level that the NMPC would perform at the strategic. They would work together to implement and coordinate at the operational level the various complex dimensions of the programs.

How Will It Work?

This component, appropriately expanded, augmented, and staffed by the same lineup of agencies that contributes staff to the NMPC, should be permanently established at each of the four regional unified commands' locations. As with the NMPC, the members would report to their respective agencies and would work with the military staffs to oversee implementation of plans and programs developed by the NMPC and to recommend programs for the NMPC to develop.

The expanded JIATF/CG would operate full-time—managing the programs in the field, at the tactical level; working on day-to-day implementation of prevention plans and programs, as well as crisis intervention and recovery and reconstruction; and providing the full spectrum links, across all dimensions, with the strategy and policy levels.

The unified commands would continue to help produce war plans. But now we would also have an interagency element to produce a prevention plan, the nonmilitary elements of an intervention plan, and a reconstruction plan; and they would help monitor the outcomes of their plans.

An expanded and augmented JIATF/CG, operating full-time at a headquarters such as CENTCOM, would have been responsible for coordinating the nonmilitary dimensions during Operation Enduring Freedom in Afghanistan and would now be coordinating development programs in that country. As the mission shifted from intervention to humanitarian aid to reconstruction, this coordination would have been critical at each stage of this process.

Defense and State Department programs, for example—as I learned when I commanded CENTCOM—don't necessarily reinforce one another. The JIATF/CG team, working the issues and implementation at the operational level, would make sure that Defense, State, and other agency programs stayed on the same track.

AT THE TACTICAL LEVEL

The tactical level is the field level—where actual actions take place on the ground.

The military brings a massive ground force to the battlefield—battalions, brigades, and squadrons. But who brings the political force to the battlefield? Who brings the economic force to the battlefield? Who brings the informational force to the battlefield? We should create a deployable capability in every one of these areas.

At the tactical level, just as at the strategic and operational levels, we must create an integrating organization to implement the strategy, the programs, and their component tools and skills. I call this organization the Inter-Agency Field Force—IAFF.

The IAFF would be a deployable, civilian capability that would join military forces in the field to handle the nonmilitary dimensions of program implementation or postconflict recovery and reconstruction.

Though it would *not* be a military organization, the field force could be structured along the lines of military reserve units. Experts with relevant skills would be contracted or assigned to participate in the program through the various agencies, who would then activate the expert personnel for exercises, training, and actual operations. The force would be modular, allowing agencies to put together teams with capabilities tailored for specific missions.

It could be administered and logistically supported by military units such as Civil Affairs commands, but the personnel would retain their chain of authority back to their parent agencies through the JIATF/CG at the operational level. It would parallel the military lines of command.

In the field, their primary job would be to build or reestablish institutions that are credible and viable and can handle the challenges thrown at them. This would include alleviating the environmental problems that created or at least enabled the instabilities.

How Will It Work?

An expert in Southeast Asian economic systems at the University of Michigan signs up for the program. While keeping his day job, he would also receive compensation and recognition from—let's say— the State Department for participating in the Field Force. And much like military reserve officers, he would join others with complementary skills to spend a few weekends and summer weeks in drills, exercises, and simulation games. The teams would be trained to handle virtually any situation developing on the ground, from a simmering conflict to a gathering crisis to intervention, recovery, and reconstruction.

To get the teams where they need to go, with all the gear and equipment they will need there, we could use already existing capabilities of the Army's Civil Affairs Command, who can provide everything from travel to secure communications to mosquito nets.

The Coalition Provisional Authority (CPA) that our government sent in to govern Iraq after our 2003 invasion was an ad hoc kluge— with no advance plans or training to do the job. Unlike its military counterpart, it was not trained, organized, and equipped for the mission. We all know the results.

The Inter-Agency Field Force would have all the skills, training, planning, and equipment needed to do that job—and many others— in every threatened country and region. It would be a field-deployable CPA-like organization.

If the IAFF had been assigned the CPA's job in Iraq, a team would have been activated virtually from the moment the president gave the go-ahead for an invasion; the team would have been briefed on all the relevant planning and would have offered appropriate inputs; it would have had a close, standing association with CENTCOM; it would have worked with the NMPC and the JIATF/CG linked to CENTCOM; it would have trained and exercised with the military;

and it would have identified beforehand the additional members and skills it would need to do the job in Iraq.

The staffing for IAFF could be drawn from retired personnel on contract, academics on contract, other civilian contractors, or others with specialized expertise. Their agreement, or contract, to mobilize in event of need and to participate in periodic exercises and scheduled training could also be incorporated into the understanding. Teams of these experts could be led by members of the departments and agencies who would maintain communications with their teams, keep them abreast of planning, events, and relevant information. The teams would be activated under administrative control of the Civil Affairs Command and their operational authority would be retained by their appropriate department or agency. They would report directly to their department or agency and inform their counterpart members on the JIATF/CG.

THE CHOICE

Obviously, in making broad recommendations for change, the devil is in the details.

The intention is not to offer these proposals as a totally worked-out program for change, but to suggest approaches to dealing with the new situations we face that may provide better alternatives to the layered, stovepiped thinking and organizing that severely limit our power and influence in today's world. Yet even as military and business experiment with and adopt innovations such as those I've offered, our government continues to add bloated bureaucracy.

We keep relearning this lesson: In today's vastly changed world, we must have true integration, responsiveness, effective planning, immediate availability of informed expertise, cooperation with international and nongovernmental organizations, and coordination of all our efforts. If we adopt any proposals in strategic thinking, organizational change, integrated planning, and on-scene execution that fail to take this lesson into account, we will continue to crash up against threats, crises, emergencies, and chaotic conditions that we won't be able to manage or control. And these will likely cascade through the globalized environment and come back to bite us where and when we least expect it.

CHAPTER NINE

ON THE FRONT LINES OF PEACE

America's foreign policy supports freedom, democracy, and human dignity for all mankind, and we make no apologies for it. The opportunity society we want for ourselves we also want for others, not because we're imposing our system on others but because those opportunities belong to all people as God-given birthrights and because by promoting democracy and economic opportunity we make peace more secure.

—Ronald Reagan, 1984

More than a century and a half ago, Alexis de Tocqueville cast a clear-eyed gaze on the essential element that gives the United States its special identity among nations. It is *not* its ethnic or religious character, it is *not* its ancient traditions and rituals. It is a set of core values.

These core values include the democracy we have developed that allows us a clear voice in our governance; the rule of law system that seeks justice for all; the market economy structure that allows fair competition, growth, and opportunity and promotes prosperity; and the protection and promotion of basic human rights established in our constitution.

Until recently, we concentrated on fully realizing these values within our own society. That defined our national course. Though we might have offered our values as a model for others, we only rarely took actions aimed at establishing our values beyond our own borders.

That course is no longer viable. We can no longer just set the example. Dangerous threats are breeding in environments where these values do not exist or where there is no capacity to gain them. It has become imperative to foster, and even to implant, our values in these environments.

We are reluctant imperialists. We don't relish imposing our systems, beliefs, and values on others. Yet we are convinced that our values are universal and that their adoption or achievement by all mankind will make a more peaceful, prosperous, and secure world. With this goal before us, we have offered our values to others . . . but with mixed results. We have not been skillful in understanding how to effectively apply our power in ways that do not alienate or threaten other societies. We understand warmaking far better than we understand peacemaking.

We must make the effort to promote stability and peace. In that way we will best promote the values we hope to share with those peoples in the world who suffer from their absence.

The reforms I proposed earlier are necessary systemic, organizational, and conceptual changes that will put us in a better position to effect true stability and peace in a world growing more unstable and threatening. Implementing these reforms will require leadership and courage, both because they are radical and because they threaten vested interests. Implementing these changes means redesigning our vision, strategy, government structure, wasteful and counterproductive practices (patronage and pork); and it means additionally participation in multinational efforts (we can no longer go it alone and solely follow our own stars).

Yet these changes are in no way unprecedented. In the past we have taken similarly bold and radical course changes. Truman and

Marshall did it after World War II. But the changes in Washington and in our systems and processes are only the first steps. They will build the foundation for bringing order to disorder. They will not in themselves bring order and peace to the world. Action out there—implementation on the ground—is critical.

Implementation with what implements?

The tools available for foxhole-level actions are many and varied.

TOOLS OF IMPLEMENTATION

These tools come in the form of negotiation and mediation to prevent or end conflict, USAID projects, teams to monitor agreements, military forces to provide security, military teams to provide training, military intervention, and dozens more. I have personally participated in all of these at the operational level, and in many of them at the foxhole level. What has struck me is the powerful array of tools available to our government and to nongovernmental organizations and international agencies. The problem is not the availability of tools; it is that they are not effectively coordinated or melded on the ground.

Let me shine a light on a pair of tools that I know well from personal experience, negotiation—and its close relatives mediation and facilitation—and capacity building.

Negotiation

The distinction between negotiation, mediation, and facilitation is less subtle in practice than it may appear in print. Though the goals they work for are similar, negotiators, mediators, and facilitators have very different functions.

Negotiation brings together contending parties in the hope of resolving through discussion the issues that separate them. In mediation, a third party brings the negotiating parties together, while participating fully in the process and offering them help in reaching an agreement. Facilitation is a subset of mediation. Facilitators are not directly involved in the negotiation; they simply aid the process. We can put the three together in any combination.

Negotiation is a science. Negotiators must master skills and techniques. They have to know the culture and the issues; avoid mindsets and preconceptions; know how to open a forum for every person and group in the process; know how to get and maintain the initiative; look for innovation and nontraditional approaches; and pay attention to the core objectives of each side, and to their grievances—without getting stuck in either their objectives or their grievances as set-in-stone end states.

But negotiation is also an art. Negotiators must have the talent and the personality for negotiating, and this talent is inherent. They have to enjoy interacting with people in confrontational and aggressive situations. They have to have a sixth sense for picking opportunities and moment. They have to be good at reading people.

The potential casting call for negotiators can be large.

Sometimes prominent international statesmen like Jimmy Carter and Nelson Mandela, or others, like Jessie Jackson, George Mitchell, or James Baker, get called as special envoys—either because of their reputation, their knowledge, their experience, or their access to other leaders, or maybe because they have a special relationship with the president.

Many and varied organizations are also available to take on the negotiating mission—international organizations such as the UN or NATO; regional political organizations such as the African Union; regional coalitions; or independent organizations (NGOs), such as the Henri Dunant Centre in Geneva or the Kroc Institute in San Diego, which are private, small, and far more flexible than the more official organizations, and which bring no baggage and offer no challenge to sovereignty. Some organizations that do similar work, such as the United States Institute of Peace in Washington, have a quasi-governmental connection in that they are funded by Congress but are independent of the government in all other respects. Each of these NGOs has its core competencies. The Dunant Centre's strength is mediation. Kroc has a strong interest in developing capacity for civil society, and they have considerable expertise in the prevention and the removal of destabilizing conditions. U.S. Institute of Peace's strength is in implementation and capacity building—and especially in building government infrastructure.

Negotiations and mediations can also get started as a result of interventions from the outside—usually by one or another of the same cast of characters. And these may be enhanced by other kinds of humanitarian operations in the areas of food, health care, shelter, rebuilding.

Nations that all sides see as "fair traders" will often be called on to help resolve conflicts: the United States, for example, has long had a central role in negotiating the Israel-Palestine dispute, because only the United States—with its influence on Israel—has a chance of success.

A set of countries around the world—primarily the Nordic countries, Canada, and Switzerland—have traditionally centered their foreign policy on peacemaking, mediation, and conflict resolution, and have funded and provided resources for these activities. (The Norwegian government, for example, is mediating the Sri Lanka conflict. The Malaysians are mediating in Mindanao.) Though their level of involvement may vary according to the political flavor of the government currently in power, these nations are always involved in peacemaking, always willing to donate money to peace efforts or implementation, host conferences, provide humanitarian and often military support (as intervenors, observers, peacekeeping forces, and the like), offer asylum, and support organizations such as the Dunant Centre.

I've participated in many negotiations and mediations. Let me share some of that experience.

For me, going out to some country as a negotiator or mediator is like a military operation: I'm given a mission or a task. To persuade the Israelis and Palestinians to take small, concrete, positive steps toward peace. Or, to defuse a dangerous and rapidly escalating confrontation in Kashmir between Pakistan and India by gaining Pakistani cooperation to pull back from Kargil, across the Line of Control, break contact with the Indians, and achieve a cease-fire. Or more generally my task has been to broker agreements or to make arrangements to implement an agreement.

At the start of a negotiation, my first priority is to come up to speed rapidly on the issues and the culture, and then to get a take on the personalities I'm dealing with. Next, I look at the structure of the process I'm involved in—or if I might have to create one. And then I try to draw out the issues as the participants themselves see them. I try to do all this without preconceptions and prejudgments. The idea is to get a fix on what is actually *there,* and not on the view through any particular lens.

The task then becomes to find ways to resolve the issues so that both sides can feel—at a minimum—that they are not going to lose if they consent to an agreement. But ideally both sides will feel that they both have won. It can't be a win-lose situation. It has to be a win-win. Or at least a no-lose/no-lose.

Many times during negotiations, the process is more important than the substance. Or perhaps more accurately, it's sometimes better to keep the process going than to break it apart over substance. Substance is often elusive (What *exactly* are they *really* fighting about?) and is almost certainly hard to deal with. So we may need time to slide into talking about it. Or else we may need to show progress, even though we know that talking about the substantial issues right now is going to get us nowhere. This means that we might have to put our— and their—focus on the process. We may need to simply keep them talking until the time is more ripe for substantial discussion.

The term "ripeness" is used frequently in conflict resolution. Most often, it refers to the moment when it hits opposing parties that they can't realistically continue their confrontation. It's the moment when they realize they have to try to work something else out.

In 2001, I was asked to help facilitate the Henri Dunant Centre's negotiations between the rebels in the oil-rich, Sumatran province of Aceh and the Indonesian government. (The Aceh rebels are seeking independence.) At one point in the negotiations, we had reached an impasse; and the government's negotiator, a retired ambassador, was frustrated. He saw this effort as a personal mission from the president, and he wanted to succeed; but the impasse had left him discouraged. He was just about ready to throw in the towel: "I need substance, and all you're giving me is process," he charged the mediators.

But at that stage of the game, process was what we needed. We hadn't yet reached the "ripeness" we needed to deal with substance. The ambassador from Jakarta was on a different timeline from that of his counterparts on the other side.

Because we didn't want to lose momentum and the positive condition we had already achieved, we created a series of minor agreements both sides could accept. None of them was a big deal; but they kept the process moving and positive.

Through all this, I felt the ambassador's pain, but we needed a little kabuki in the process in order to keep moving forward.

In the end the rebels and the central government signed an agreement . . . that was later broken . . . and was later renegotiated. . . . That's the way these things work. We have to be *very* patient and look at the long term.

Soon after I retired from the Marine Corps, I was asked by the State Department, the Henri Dunant Centre, the United States Institute of Peace (USIP), and other similar organizations to bring my dual experience as warrior-peacemaker to their efforts at conflict resolution and mediation. My firsthand knowledge of war and combat and of negotiation and mediation offered a perspective they found unusual and valuable. Negotiators don't often have combat experience; and military officers with extensive combat experience have only rarely been involved in serious peacemaking negotiations.

In 2001, the State Department asked me to help mediate the Israeli-Palestinian conflict. In the resulting talks, we managed to bring the two sides a little closer together . . . until a wave of Palestinian suicide bombings in the spring of 2002 killed the process. Meanwhile, the Henri Dunant Centre in Geneva had asked me to participate in the ongoing negotiations in Aceh and the United States Institute of Peace had asked me to help with negotiations to end the Moro rebellion in Mindanao in the Philippines. I am still actively involved in these talks.

In the course of the negotiations, I have traveled to the front lines in rebel areas of Aceh and Mindanao. I've talked to rebel leaders face-to-face on their home turf . . . and sometimes in their homes. Lessons I first learned in Vietnam once again drove me out to the front lines, this time into the jungles of Mindanao and Sumatra, jungles that achingly reminded me of Vietnam—rice paddies, water buffalos, farmers in wide-brimmed conical straw hats, children in shorts.

If we're going to convince insurgents out there that we are interested in them as human beings and that we actually take them seriously and are willing to treat them with respect, then we have to meet them on their home territory. We have to listen to their goals and concerns. Sometimes they make a very good case. Sometimes they're looking for pie in the sky.

Without that face-to-face listening, it's hard to gain trust.

How many foreign-policy experts, policymakers, and even diplomats in Washington have actually seen the face of an "enemy"? How many have sat down with a terrorist? How many have met an insurgent, a rebel, a revolutionary, or even anyone who wears the uniform of a "hostile military force"? Anyone who *has,* and who has come to understand who they *really* are, where they *really* come from, and how their goals grow out of their own environments, will be a far more powerful negotiator.

That is *not* to say that knowing is forgiving. I don't buy that fallacy. Understanding may bring revulsion and contempt. Knowing evil doesn't make evil less evil. Sitting down at a table with insurgents doesn't guarantee my sympathy for them or for their cause. Some of them perform acts that we can never accept. Some evil is absolute; it puts the evildoer beyond the pale. We *absolutely* can't deal with some people.

Yet, on the flip side, rebel and insurgent movements are never monolithic. They always have factions. Both the Free Aceh Movement and the Moro Liberation Front are in a struggle that plays out at many levels. A faction fighting solely for independence and a better life might coexist—maybe comfortably, maybe uncomfortably—with a faction that's much closer to tipping over the radical terrorist edge. The more moderate voices are reluctant to get tangled up in international, radical movements: "That's not the way we want to go. It's not what our movement is about."

We have to be careful not to mix the factions together.

♌

My participation in the Philippines peacemaking process started in 2003.

The process itself began in 1996. That year, in an attempt to settle the decades-long guerrilla war in Mindanao, Philippines President Ramos reached agreement with the Moro National Liberation Front (MNLF) granting a degree of autonomy and other concessions. A number of incentives had been offered to the MNLF—some from the Philippine government, and some that the government couldn't provide . . . but which the United States could.

The United States Agency for International Development (USAID) was then brought in to operate what turned out to be a brilliant and highly successful Arms for Farms program. Guerrillas who came in out of the field and gave up their weapons received farm equipment and training in exchange, either in their home villages or wherever they chose to settle. USAID also built facilities for drying and processing their produce and silos for storing it; and they actually launched varieties of crops that were new to the Moros *as well as* new markets for them. The Japanese have a high demand for seaweed (a major food source), and the demand was then higher than the supply; Mindanao is rich in bays, inlets, and lagoons—all ideal for seaweed cultivation. Though the Moros had no experience in seaweed farming, USAID taught them how to do it. The new crop paid off.

The result: USAID's success rate for bringing MNLF guerrillas out of the field and providing them with sufficient work to support families is in the neighborhood of 96 to 98 percent. In other words, only a tiny fraction returned to the jungle and the guerrilla bands . . . a good old-fashioned capitalist success story. The market worked.

Not every element in the 1996 settlement worked so well. Both the MNLF and the Philippine government failed to live up to all their commitments, while a significant part of the Moro people, seeing the accommodation as a sellout, split off from the MNLF, called themselves the Moro Islamic Liberation Front (MILF), and continued to fight.

After the Philippine presidency passed to Gloria Arroyo, the new president reached out to the MILF and the discussions made good progress. The Malaysians then agreed to mediate the continuing negotiations. They set up committees to deal with incidents and put international monitors on the ground (from Brunei and Malaysia; others were scheduled to arrive from Bahrain); they set up local autonomous zones where there would be no government presence unless there was some violent provocation or other serious rationale; and in general, they reached out to the MILF. (Some of these arrangements had been part of the original agreement with the MNLF.) A shaky cease-fire came into effect.

Meanwhile, President Arroyo asked President Bush to add American help to the peace process, and Bush came through with two programs. USAID offered to extend its economic incentive programs—like Arms for Farms—to the MILF. And the USIP was asked to get involved—but sensitively, in a very low-key way that complemented the Malaysians' mediation efforts. The Malaysians had to be in charge. Malaysians, like the Moros, are Muslims; the MILF trusted Malaysians more than they trusted Americans. Therefore, the USIP's role became to facilitate—with social issues, with building legal institutions and the rule of law, and with helping to research ancestral domain issues.

Many years ago the Philippine government launched what might be called an ethnic management program. Thousands of Filipinos from the Christian north were transported south to Mindanao in an attempt to drive the Moros from their land and weight the population in favor of Christians. These Christians have now been on Mindanao for generations. The original Moro inhabitants had been illegally deprived of their property. The USIP was asked to help resolve that thorny issue of ancestral domain.

The USIP came to me particularly for my expertise in monitoring and implementation of cease-fire agreements, but they also asked me to look at broader issues. I then went out to look at the situation on the ground and meet with the leadership of the MILF. Before that meeting, I met separately with the very competent Malaysian monitoring team which was headed by a Malaysian general. Then I was joined by Gene Martin, a retired diplomat from the State Department and former deputy chief of mission at our embassy in Manila, who now worked at the USIP.

Gene Martin and I met with fifteen of the senior and more moderate MILF leaders at a small conference center outside Cotobato, the capital of Mindanao. It was an exploratory meeting. We were there to explain what the USIP hoped to bring to the peace process, to give the MILF leaders ideas about how we might help, and to get their views of where things stood.

We knew we were facing people who would not unconditionally welcome us. They appreciated American help and would hear us out—but warily; their history with us has not been positive; the level of trust was low. Americans don't automatically walk in and instill a great sense of warmth.

A hundred years ago, after we drove Spain out of the Philippines, Moros fought us for their independence; their great-grandfathers fought our great-grandfathers in the same Mindanao jungles where Moro guerrillas fight today.

At one point we took a break outside on the lawn, where an old brass cannon was mounted. Somebody waved a hand at it: "This is what we shot at you a hundred years ago," he said with a laugh. They're still looking for independence . . . and they remain uncertain about our real intentions.

They're even less sure that the Philippine government will deliver in the long run. They have not been encouraged by the government's previous failures to comply with agreements.

My aim was therefore to connect personally with them and show them a different side of America than they had seen before. I wanted them to know that I cared about them, yet recognized our conflicted history with each other. And finally, I wanted to assure them that that didn't have to continue, nor would it prevent us from helping them.

The personal connection went well. The first evening I was invited to a wedding; and after the celebration and reception, I ate dinner with one of the leaders in his home.

But this was, of course, only an introduction . . . at best a modest beginning. They accepted us for who we were. But they still had questions and doubts about our relationship with the government— their enemy. Because of our troubled historical relationship, they surely wondered how much we would actually be prepared to help *them.* They likely suspected that we were the government's broker and on the government's side. That was a natural reaction.

The same thing happened when I mediated between Israelis and Palestinians. Every Palestinian and every Arab automatically assumes that any American who walks in to mediate a situation is in there as Israel's broker. The mediator has to gain trust from both sides and continually demonstrate his neutrality in the mediation process. He must continually take the pulse of each side to ensure that misperceptions of bias have not set in.

In our meetings with the MILF leaders, we discussed at length issues of concern to everyone involved.

For the MILF, the ultimate dream is independence; but since they recognized that independence was unlikely anytime soon, they seemed willing to accept real local autonomy, including genuine respect for their uniqueness, their culture, and their religion. And they likewise expected economic development, education programs, health programs, and some resolution of ancestral domain issues.

For the government, the immediate concern was a strong suspicion—strongly denied by the MILF leadership—that the organization had ties with Jamaah Islamiya and other international terrorist groups. We asked tough questions about this association, making it clear that any such links would make our help and involvement at best problematic. "If you get involved with groups on the terrorist list," we explained, "or find yourselves on that list, we can't do you much good."

They continued to plead innocent.

The choice faced by separatist groups such as those in Mindanao and Aceh is a big one. Will they go for stability and peace or for links with international terrorism and possibly unending violence?

In my own view, Al Qaeda, Jamaah Islamiya, and the other radical groups see these separatist groups as crucial centers of gravity in their global war to create an Islamist utopia. Bringing them into their camp would be a great victory; they work hard at proselytizing and persuasion.

The majority of separatist leaders, however, are reluctant to join the radicals. The radicals are *too* extreme; the radical approach threatens to destroy their own intent and their own identity; and a radical association that puts their own organizations on the terrorist list has a grim downside. At the same time, they don't want to cut the radicals off absolutely. They are, after all, brother Muslims; and they sympathize with some of their Islamist visions. So they try to keep the radicals at a distance without totally disconnecting from them.

Meanwhile, radical groups do influence some of the young fighters. Frustrated, radicalized, and captivated by Islamist glamour, they fall for the siren lure of the song of Osama bin Laden: "Join our cause. It is an Islamic cause. It is a global cause. We are Islamic peoples fighting to restore the ancient and authentic majesty of Islam." And so they link up with Al Qaeda, Jamaah Ismaliya, or Abu Sayaf. To the young fighters, the Al Qaeda program is the only promise left that might work: "Our people have struggled for decades, and we're still getting nowhere. Osama has a vision. He sees a future worth fighting and dying for."

All the separatist groups are going through a tremendous internal struggle over these questions. Both the answers to these questions and the resolution of these struggles have become vitally important. A significant part of the battle for peace will be determined by the choice these groups make. That's why we *must* wade in and deal with them now.

Although freedom fighters sometimes do horrific things, that does not necessarily mean that the organizations they follow have become radicalized, fanatical, religious terrorist groups *yet*. But they could go that way. In both Mindanao and Aceh, the causes the rebels are fighting for are not going to go away soon; and the seeming failure to make progress in resolving their outstanding grievances can leave them feeling discouraged, frustrated, and repressed . . . and open to becoming radicalized. Without some kind of progress—in mediation, in peacemaking, in reform, in building a stable environment, in building capacities—we risk losing them.

The issues then become: "How can we generate the changes they so desperately want, and in ways that are acceptable to them and that preserve the essential cultural aspects of their lives? How can we do all that so as not to create greater instabilities than we have now? And how can we do it quickly enough to satisfy their urgency?"

Capacity Building

The measure of successful on-the-ground programs is greater capacity leading to increased stability. Obviously, there's a lot of technical skill involved—as we have already seen in USAID's Arms for Farms program in Mindanao, and as I learned during my time as commander of U.S. Central Command.

I stepped into my tour as commander in chief of CENTCOM with the knowledge that I was facing a volatile and crisis-prone part of the world, of vital importance for energy and resources, and that the disorder, instabilities, and conflicts in the region were likely to present our nation with ever more dangerous crises in the near future.

Iraq had been a running sore since its invasion of Kuwait. Iran had been a running sore since 1979. The Taliban was ruling Afghanistan. Even then, we were aware that Al Qaeda was dangerous; and it was not the only Islamist organization that gave us concerns. Terrorists in Egypt had recently killed Western tourists. Yemen was trying to stabilize itself after coming out of a terrible civil war, but faced serious frictions with the other countries of the region. There were internal instabilities in almost every country. And every country had a border dispute with some neighbor or other. Somalia remained a failed state. There was an ongoing civil war in Sudan. Ethiopia and Eritrea had a longstanding and often violent border dispute. There were border tensions in the Caspian between the Iranians and the

Russians—with oil as the prize. Pakistan and India remained in conflict, with constant flare-ups over Kashmir. There were even problems in otherwise idyllic places like the Seychelles, where Asian fishing fleets were poaching their waters. Everywhere there was smuggling and the drug trade. Everywhere I looked I could see dangerous instabilities.

My first question: "Can I do anything about this?"

Obviously, I had a direct responsibility as commander to manage the conflicts and crises that might involve our military. Yet, I was also trying to find ways to minimize our own direct military interventions in these crises. How do we avoid putting our own boots on the ground?

Simple answer: We don't intervene in a crisis when there is no crisis.

Next question: How do we prevent crises?

The answer to that question presented an even greater challenge: we had to build order and stability that might head off conflicts and crises before they hurt us or anybody else. I started looking at what we could do here and now to move this crisis-prone region toward greater stability.

We had a choice. We could sit back in a secure location like a fireman, wait for the alarm, and then rush off to put the fire out. Or we could move out into the neighborhood and locate all the fire hazards—the piles of dead undergrowth, the flammable materials stored unsafely—and then get rid of them.

My experience with crisis intervention had begun in northern Iraq and continued in Somalia. In both, we came in as firemen. It hit me in Somalia that that didn't have to be so.

When we moved into Somalia, it was already a failed state. It had crashed from instability to chaos. Yet even then, Somalia's problems were not intractable. The nation could have been salvaged. But I kept asking myself: "What if we had gone in earlier? If we had taken on Somalia when the first serious signs of instability appeared—or when we heard from people we trusted in the region that Somalia was in danger of exploding—could we have managed the situation better?"

This burr stayed under my saddle.

When I came to command CENTCOM and had the ability to choose between fighting fires or preventing them, I chose prevention. I did not intend to sit back and say, "Hey, my job is purely military. When you're ready to send me in, coach, that's when I go in." If there was any possible approach to making this a less crisis-prone, more secure and stable region, I wanted to try it.

My challenge: "What's the best approach? What can we promote, invest in, and support?"

My conclusion: "Regionalization."

I recognized that no single nation in the region was capable of coping with area instabilities. But could we create regional capabilities to cope with them? That is, could we build and support regional coalitions of friendly nations who could cooperatively take on local instabilities? And since it would be *their* commitment to building stability, they would own it and feel responsible for it. And since they were not outsiders in the region (as we were), there would be greater acceptance of their presence there.

Obviously, they would need our help. Whatever we invested in these projects would pay off later in regional stability, order, and peace. It was far better to invest a little now than pay a lot later to end a crisis.

CENTCOM was already building cooperative security capacity in the region—training, technical assistance, equipment—but the regional nations had a long, long way to travel before they reached the kind of real collective security that we had in, say, NATO. Yet, it was worth making a start in that direction.

Since even tentative steps on that road made all the regional nations very uneasy, I wondered if we could help in other areas. "Can we make a positive difference in other dimensions?" I asked myself. "And in that way build momentum for closer cooperation on security?"

Every nation in the region had border disputes and other political differences with their neighbors. If we could help them find ways to resolve their border disputes, could we then help them cooperate on other thorny issues, like water use?

In that part of the world, water can cause wars. Turkey and Syria have come close to war over water. Kyrgyzstan and Uzbekistan have had water problems. Egypt has clearly told Sudan that interfering with the sources of the Nile will be countered with force. The Nile defines Egypt. In the Persian Gulf, desalination is the lifeblood of the coastal populations. If the gulf were to be contaminated—by a major oil spill, for example, or by sabotage—the effects could be catastrophic.

Could easing these kinds of environmental frictions lead to greater military cooperation? It was worth a try.

Regionalization became an essential component of the regional strategy that it was my job as CINC to produce.

The Clinton administration both gave backing to this challenge and added to it. Their approach to building international order and stability was called engagement: direct, peaceful, multifaceted, and multilateral involvement in other countries. (Other administrations have used other terms as they pursued similar goals.) Secretary of Defense William Cohen then translated engagement into a military context by authorizing the CINCs to "shape the environment": we were encouraged to create favorable conditions in countries of interest to us. "Let's look at the future," he advised us. "What can we do now that can have a positive influence later?" This was very controversial, not in the least because it involved us in *more* than military activities and operations.

My ability—or power—to launch the initiatives I had in mind went back to the revolutionary 1986 Goldwater-Nichols Act.

The act did not itself create the powerful regional CINCs we have today, but they evolved from the changes mandated by the legislation. The unified commands in the context of the Cold War were all about warfighting or the preparations for warfighting. The Goldwater-Nichols act created a new kind of operational regional command and gave the regional commanders much greater authority. But until the fall of the Berlin Wall, the regional commands were still primarily seen in a military operational sense.

In the 1990s, the Clinton administration added another role to the unified commands. In addition to their warfighting role and their preparations for war, the regional commands would expand to become an instrument of implementing policy. Out of this came the key part CINCs were to play in the administration's multilateral approach. The CINCs were given the authority to take our regional strategies much farther than ever before: not only to shape the environment but—more loosely—to take that task beyond the military dimension. And our regional CINCs—General Charles Wilhelm (CINC of Southern Command: Latin America), Admiral Dennis Blair (CINC of Pacific Command), General Wesley Clark (CINC of European Command and the NATO commander), and me—grasped what we were being asked to do, and began to work out how to do it. We all launched initiatives aimed at what I called regionalization, though the others had their own names for it.

We all worked to find collective approaches to stabilizing our regions. We all took a hard look at regional instabilities, and we did what we could to fix them. During this process, we all became more closely engaged with our diplomatic counterparts—the ambassadors, the regional desks and bureaus at the State Department.

But the CINCs inevitably became the central focus of these efforts—we had more resources; we had more forces on the ground; we had more local connections; and we spent more time in the regions actually engaged in working on the problems. Very often we were dealing with leaders who came out of their nations' military services (rare among our own political leadership), which made it easier for them to relate to us than to diplomats. That gave us more of a base in the region.

As I embarked on this process, I was greatly encouraged by the region's leaders. In my early visits, I tried to approach them openly and with humility, and to simply listen without the usual American know-it-all arrogance that tells them what they ought to be doing. When my key question came: "What do you see as our role here?" Their invariable answer was: "*Stability.* The United States, more than any other factor, can take actions to make this region more stable. But you can also take actions that are tremendously destabilizing—maybe without intending it." They were essentially asking us not to come on in the region like the 800-pound gorilla—a role we all too easily fall into. Yet our power and influence there—correctly applied—could bring greater stability and peace. (This was of course before 9/11 and our 2003 invasion of Iraq.)

My task as CINC was to develop a strategy to achieve the stability they hoped for. And I didn't want it to be a nicely bound, beautifully designed, show-and-tell document. I wanted it to be a living thing that we could adapt to changing circumstances.

An important element in my developing strategy was to build up the security capabilities of the Gulf Cooperation Council (GCC—the Gulf regional security coalition of Saudi Arabia, the United Arab Emirates, Bahrain, Oman, Qatar, and Kuwait). I knew this was going to be difficult. Multilateral cooperation did not come easy to the members of the GCC. In fact, bilateral cooperation with the United States often came easier. That often made us and not the GCC the glue in the region. In the long run, that wasn't to their advantage or to ours. I hoped to make the GCC the glue and to move us into a support role.

The slender levels of cooperation in the GCC come out of the historical evolution of the states, whose development has followed a different path from ours or Europe's. After World War II, the U.S. and Europe were confronted by an expanding and hungry Soviet Union.

Collective security proved to be an effective and lasting counter to this threat. The American- and European-designed NATO evolved into the greatest military coalition in history. The Arab states of the Persian Gulf are not yet ready for that kind of coalition.

Enlightenment on this subject came to me early in my tour as CENTCOM commander, during a conversation with an ambassador to the United States from the region. "Why does the GCC seem unable to turn into a strong regional structure like NATO or the EU?" I asked him.

"You know," he explained, "we put on this face of Arab brotherhood and unity. But it's only a face. We're all very different from each other.

"You have to understand where we are in our history," he continued. "You're expecting us to act like the Europe at the end of the twentieth century. But that's not where we are. We're more like Europe at the beginning of the twentieth century. We don't yet have much trust and confidence in each other."

He was right. The more time I spent traveling through the nations of the region, the more I came to understand how remarkably different they are from each other. The history of Arab nations after World War II will tell you how difficult it has been to create an Arab coalition. Powerful, charismatic leaders such as Egypt's Nasser tried it and failed.

The ambassador also made me realize the most important key to regionalization—the nations have to be ready for it. There has to be ripeness.

Convincing Europe to build a cooperative regional identity and a regional capability before World War I—or in its aftermath—would have been unthinkable. Can anyone imagine Britain, Germany, France, Italy, or the Austro-Hungarian Empire getting together under the conditions that existed then? They would have locked up in an asylum anyone suggesting it.

They were ready for it after World War II.

Two world wars had shattered Europe. Europeans were desperate to prevent the recurrence of those tragedies. They created the European Union. Yet that did not spring into existence fully developed. It began very simply with the European Coal and Steel Community. The trust and cooperation built up from there.

Regional coalitions don't just happen because regionalization is a lovely idea. The nations have to be ready for it. They've got to build it from some small base that doesn't make any of them nervous. From this seed, trust and cooperation may grow.

If we were going to build regional capability, I concluded, we had to lead off with smaller programs that would build trust.

Surprisingly—and serendipitously—as I was starting to work on these issues, the GCC nations had already begun to resolve some of their longstanding political differences on their own initiative. A particularly nasty dustup had encouraged the Saudis and the Yemenis to resolve their border issues; the Yemenis also resolved their border issue with the Omanis; and the Omanis, the UAE, Qatar, and Bahrain put a tense border dispute up for international arbitration, then accepted the results.

The resolution of these differences ignited momentum for what I planned to do next: find nonthreatening ways to encourage them to work together . . . and to work as a coherent entity with us. But my ultimate goal was to shape them into a viable collective security arrangement. I wanted them to work together for their mutual defense. I wanted them to exercise together (their combined exercises were that in name only), and I wanted them to have the same military standards, an integrated command and control system, and combined and focused capabilities. And when the time came, I wanted their militaries be able to fight together. In those days they had none of that. Without it they could not effectively deter and deal with the regional hegemons who threaten stability.

I knew I was not going to achieve wonderful results quickly. Attempting that leap in a single move was never going to work. I had to come up with a program we could undertake together that they could collectively support. I wanted an issue on which there would be no disputes—an issue so benign, so innocuous, so nonthreatening, and so agreeable that they could not possibly argue over it. And I wanted to give them positive reasons to work together.

Though water sources are a potential source of conflict in the region, the GCC members have very powerful incentives to cooperate over water. They all take much of their water from the Persian Gulf, and they all depend on desalination plants to make it drinkable. They would all benefit from cooperating to protect the gulf. If, for example, the Iranians were ever to decide to attack the Arabs, one of their first actions would likely be to pollute those waters and take out the desalination plants. They are strategically vital to the states along the gulf.

So the first issue I chose was water.

Once again, my ultimate goal had nothing to do with whether or not they cooperated over water. That was the entry point, the easy one, the Coal and Steel Community. The issue was *not* water. It was cooperation.

We arranged regional environmental conferences focused on water issues. Representatives from the GCC came, and we brought experts in from the States—from the EPA and other U.S. agencies. We discussed shared experiences, issues, and problems; and we looked at various capabilities and technologies—evolving desalination technology, handling hazardous waste material, monitoring cleanups, taking preventive measures during disposal. We looked at efforts we could take cooperatively, like combined exercises, or cooperatively organizing ourselves to control and contain an oil spill or other contamination. We talked about our own military training and policies—the U.S. military is expected to be a good steward of the environment; this could be a model for their militaries.

The environmental conferences were a great success; they loved them and wanted to continue them. That success provided us with our springboard for the next stage of our program, which was air defense.

The biggest threat in the region was the proliferation of missiles. Except for Saudi Arabia, the GCC was a collection of tiny countries. On their own, they could do very little to stop missiles or aircraft. Aircraft and missiles fly fast, crossing three or four GCC nations in minutes. They badly needed missile and air defense . . . and not the separate systems for each nation they already had, but a collective system; and they knew it.

Even so, the cooperative air defense missile program was a tougher sell than the environment. I knew it was going to be more of a stretch for them.

We had to do this without defining a specific threat. There was no desire to antagonize potential enemies or engage in a political debate because of the differing views of the threat.

I quickly reassured them: "I'm talking about a *defensive* system," I explained. "We're going to set this up *absent* a threat. We're not pointing a gun at anybody. And we won't talk about threats, so we won't put you on the spot with your neighbors.

"Look, the United States has troops on the ground. We want to defend our troops. You want to protect your own citizens. We need to work together; and we can't work this out in the huddle when missiles are flying."

They thought about that, and essentially bought the argument . . . but then they came back at me: "Wait a minute, wait a minute. This is all a cover. Your true agenda is selling us American military equipment. You want to sell us Patriots"—air defense missiles.

And I reassured them again: "I'm not selling you anything. I'm offering our cooperation. You bring to the table whatever you have, I don't care what. British system? Hangover Soviet system? French system? We'll make it work. You don't have to buy anything to bring this thing together. We'll find a way to intercommunicate and interact. We'll take care of everything we need to make it work."

By then they were really interested. But there were still hurdles.

We have several technologically advanced early warning systems—like AWACS and satellites. It was not going to be easy for us to share this technology. But it was the heart of our own air defense; and without it, theirs would be woefully incomplete. And they knew it.

"If you're really serious with us," they told me, "you'll share early warning with us."

I agreed with them. If this effort was more than a game to encourage them to play happily together in the same sandbox, we had to go all the way with them. And I think they expected that we would fail to make that leap of faith.

But I could not make that decision on my own. It had to come from Defense Secretary Cohen. Even though the Pentagon had serious reservations over shared early warning, he cleared it and we were able to offer it to them. He saw the risks, but was willing to accept them if they resulted in greater cooperation and collective security.

His okay shocked my GCC friends. They had never imagined that we would actually go that far in trusting them. (As we started working closer with some of these countries, intelligence sharing also became important at levels that needed approval from above. Cohen and his staff were also very forthcoming in assisting this.)

My interest in this was to create an atmosphere of cooperation that could help deal with other destabilizing factors in a collective way.

MAKING IT WORK ON THE FRONT LINES

We have already seen how our fragmented, uncoordinated approach to developing and implementing policies and programs blocks our ability to accomplish our aims and goals in the world, and how perceptions of nations, societies, or specific problems often differ from agency to agency or from Congress to administration. One wants engagement. One wants sanctions. One wants to shape and invest in a major way. One wants minimal contact with minimal resources applied. The State Department will have its programs and policies. The Defense Department will have theirs. Other government agencies will have theirs—all differing significantly in philosophy, application, and allocation of resources.

These efforts can also be restricted or directed by single-issue proponents in congress who legislate broad actions based on a narrow understanding that is at odds with the views of the administration in power and of those in the foxholes. If a political decision maker is a strong proponent of an issue such as nonproliferation, human rights, or political reform, or is influenced by a strong political lobby, he or she may create or influence policies that restrict all American activities in a nation or even in a region. These restrictive, negative policies often block progress in other areas that we have strong reasons to promote. This lack of cohesiveness and common objectives results in a cacophony of activities on the ground.

I saw this as the CENTCOM commander: Decisions on military-to-military connections were constantly dialed up or down like a thermostat in response to lobbying influences or issues unrelated to security. There was no recognition of the differences between the components and the institutions we were dealing with.

If the police in some country in the region commit a human rights violation, while the military is clean and shows real progress, why punish the military? Blanket decisions or policies that don't take into account such complexities lead to unsophisticated actions that are counterproductive and frustrating for those of us on the ground who have a clearer view of the situation.

Because of this blanket approach, restrictions were placed on our military relationships with countries like Kenya, Turkmenistan, and Pakistan. We held the militaries in these places accountable for actions taken by the political leadership or by other institutions that the military did not affect.

We have likewise missed opportunities to partner with international, regional, and local agencies, nongovernmental agencies, and private sector organizations active on the ground working toward the objectives we seek to achieve. Other untapped partners—such as American businesses active in a region—could also easily be incorporated into our efforts. In my experience, business leaders have always seemed willing and anxious to develop that kind of relationship.

When we are out on the front lines, it is frustrating to discover these groups on the ground. Most of the time we share the same intentions and objectives; yet we duplicate efforts, or even compete. We confuse those we are trying to help with disjointed approaches and assets on the ground working from different perspectives. These failures offer opportunities to those who do not want us to succeed to play us off against each other and exploit the already existing friction.

Why couldn't we have planned together before we all arrived at the scene? Cooperation would obviously produce greater synergy and efficiency.

No place on earth has simple problems that lend themselves to simple solutions or single-dimension approaches. The skillful blending and application of all our elements of power, the cooperative participation of partners in implementation, and the full understanding of the complexities and nuances of the situation are absolutely necessary to put together the right policies and programs and, most importantly, to effectively implement them.

Our implementation organizations on the ground in a complex environment—post-Saddam Iraq, for example—would need this kind of depth of planning and understanding to achieve success.

Too frequently we have applied simplistic and ad hoc approaches to complex problems. Though we can't prepare for all contingencies and be prescient enough to have a plan, program, or policy for every situation, we can have highly prepared and knowledgeable entities like the National Monitoring and Planning Center (NMPC), the Joint Inter-Agency Task Force / Coordination Group (JIATF/CG), and the Inter-Agency Field Force (IAFF) ready to act. Our problem is not the creation of tools or the cost of creating tools. There are many tools available. We just need to pull them together in a cohesive way.

CULTURE WARS

After Germany and Japan surrendered in 1945, the defeated, compliant societies were relatively easy to mold. Such change is normally not that easy to accomplish.

Gaining stability is not a simple matter of building capacity. Friction comes from distrust, fear, or uncertainty. Those with vested interest in the status quo or in other outcomes will resist change. Yet, the strongest resistance normally originates in the cultural differences that create seemingly incompatible prisms through which the various parties see the issues. Culture is formed by history and geography; it generates the customs, beliefs, social forms, and material traits of a society. Too often, we fail to analyze and understand these factors. Instead, we use our own cultural prisms to determine how things should be done and in what order. We use them to assume superiority and right in all issues. We use them to stereotype and generalize. At best, this failure causes us serious problems in the world. At worst it leads to conflicts, chaos, and wars.

On a recent visit to the United States, President Musharraf of Pakistan met with our president. (I know Musharraf well, and I have great respect for him.) The first issue on Musharraf's agenda was the Middle East peace process—the Israeli-Palestinian dispute—an issue far from number one with President Bush, who, I'm sure, wanted to focus on Pakistan's role in supporting the United States in the war on terrorism.

I'm equally sure that President Musharraf is committed to providing his country's support for that effort. Yet, he is also painfully aware that making good on his commitment depends on progress in the Middle East peace process. Without that progress, you can kiss goodbye to popular support in Pakistan for the United States. If President Musharraf is to stand a chance at delivering to President Bush the U.S. president's top priority, Musharraf needs the popular support that can only be generated by eliminating a contentious issue that provokes a sense of injustice among his Muslim constituency.

But the obstacles Musharraf faces in delivering support in the war on terror do not stop there. He also faces other contentious issues at home, ranging from concerns about home-grown extremists to economic problems, government corruption, relations with India, and many more. His ability to work on our number-one priority depends on the stability that can be achieved through resolving these other issues.

We can't expect to get from Pakistan the effort needed to deal with the threat we see as most dangerous to us unless the complex issues that drive instability in Pakistan are resolved enough to permit Pakistan to act on that threat.

To make a difficult situation even more difficult, we must rebuild trust in a society still bitter over what they see as past abandonment and isolation by the United States. Pakistanis see us as having left them in the lurch after the cooperation they provided during the Afghan-Soviet War . . . not to mention their unhappiness over the economic sanctions we placed on Pakistan after they developed nuclear weapons. Progress could be further complicated by other negative issues such as control of weapons of mass destruction technology and restrictions on security assistance programs.

All these complexities and subtleties have to be woven into policies and sets of programs aimed at reaching our goals. It's clear that greater understanding and dialogue are necessary for all sides to work through the complex maze of interrelated issues that affect even the simplest and clearest objectives in cross-cultural interactions.

As I travel throughout the Middle East asking what it would take to stabilize the region and its individual nations, I hear a litany of issues. Invariably the discussion on the Arab side starts something like this:

"The United States must commit fully to the Israel-Palestine peace process. It must clearly be involved in the mediation and bring its power to bear on both sides to reach resolution.

"We must meanwhile work together to establish (or in some cases to reestablish) solid relationships that provide mechanisms for dealing with mutual security and economic issues.

"The United States has been pressing hard for rapid reform in economics and governance in the region. We agree with the goals, though we can't accept the pressure for haste. If there is to be any chance to achieve the reforms your government so fervently desires, the United States must improve its image on our streets and develop a greater appreciation for the cultural issues and frictions that block its efforts. Open criticism of our regimes and policies make it more difficult for us to cooperate on issues important to you. More care and consultation is necessary."

An American might reply like this: "You must take more actions against extremists and put more emphasis on political, economic, and social reform. You must be more cooperative on energy issues to ensure the economies of nations that depend on your energy resources are not adversely affected by price and production decisions. You must take a stronger stand against regional hegemonies that threaten stability."

The Arab reply: "We can't do these things until you deal with my concerns. You must improve your image. You must demonstrate your commitment to resolving conflicts in the region. You must temper your use of force or else you will conjure up images of the Crusaders and colonizers. You must help us with our security and economic concerns. Accomplishing these goals will empower us to move on your issues."

And the American retort: "We can't take action on those goals unless you move more dramatically to accomplish the goals we have laid out for you. We can't get support from our own people and leaders unless there is clear indication of progressive action now."

And so it would go on, back and forth, with each side certain of its own position and righteousness, and each side unyielding.

Who's going to give way first? How much trust can we afford or gain support for? How much risk can we take?

And yet we both have the same objectives. We all want peace and stability. We define the routes to get there differently.

So where do we go from here?

SETTING THE COURSE AHEAD

The keys to success on the ground are, first and foremost, a single, coordinated policy that guides the development of integrated programs. These integrated programs must have assigned resources, clear objectives, articulated actions, and assigned responsibilities that lead to the goals of our policy. The policy should involve and include partners from international, regional, local, and private organizations. It should be predicated upon a comprehensive assessment of the conditions that generate the instabilities that threaten peace and prosperity, and a clear understanding of the cultural and social issues that affect implementation of the policy. Finally, there must be a continuous dialogue and consultation with local authorities, our own decision makers, and our partners. This would provide the framework currently absent in the development and implementation of policies.

CHAPTER TEN

THE BATTLE
FOR PEACE

Peace is not merely a distant goal that we seek, but a means by which we arrive at that goal.

—Dr. Martin Luther King Jr., 1967

When the superpowers' big standoff ended, most of us in the first world took comfort in the belief that life was about to get a lot easier. No more fears of nuclear doom. No more fears of total, world-convulsing violence. No more absolute, iron-walled division between free peoples and totalitarian slave states. No more either/or global competition between communism and capitalism. Democracy and market economies had won. Everybody was free. And everybody on the planet heaved an enormous sigh of relief. Now we could all look forward to a long era of calm, peace, prosperity, and progressive growth.

We're still waiting.

What will it take to achieve true world peace?

During all my years of military service, but especially during my three years in command of CENTCOM, I've seen a lot of societies in disarray. I've seen a lot of turmoil and conflict. I've seen a lot of pain and suffering. I've seen the turmoil in one nation leap over borders and whip up turbulence hundreds or even thousands of miles from the original source. And I've seen that the first world is not immune to the turmoil—as we all learned on 9/11, in Madrid in March 2004, and in London in July 2005. And I've seen my own country and the rest of the developed world continue to keep as much distance as possible between ourselves and the unstable world. Deliberately out of sight, deliberately out of mind.

I have looked at the instability, violence, and chaos that had previously played out in places so remote they could never affect us. We had always safely ignored such conditions. We can no longer do that safely. The chain between initial cause and final outcome is so long and often so obscure that we rarely understand the connection between the pain we end up feeling and the initial wound that sparked it. But the connection is there.

We're no longer immune from the festering problems of the "other" world. We can no longer refuse to invest in preventing or resolving them. If we are going to achieve a true and lasting peace in *all* the world—a peace that guarantees security for the developed world as well as for the so-called Zone of Conflict—we can't just look after ourselves and ignore them. We will have to work hard to eliminate the instability, chaos, and violence out there.

What would it take to bring true peace?

I've been on the front lines of enough wars and seen enough violence to know that true peace is *not* passive, *not* a state of passivity. It is *not* a state of tranquility or of calm. It is not an absence of disturbance. It is not an absence of any kind. It's a presence, an action. You've got to make it happen. You've got to work at it all the time. You can't just float or tread water; you've got to swim.

Nor is peace the natural state of a society, a society's default position. It's not a state of nature—an Eden of pleasure and plenty on some lush, tropical island. It's a human construct, just as an education system is a human construct . . . just as war is a human construct.

A peaceful society will be alive. It will be charged with activity and energy. It will be dynamic. We'll see there a developing middle class and growing prosperity. There will be order and security, and a rule of law. All the other institutions—like police and health care—will be solid. Corruption will be minimal. People will find satisfaction in their personal, cultural, ethnic, or religious identities, yet the institutions of the society will be robust enough to minimize frictions between different kinds of identity. Conflicts will be dealt with through civil institutions, not violence. The media will be alive and feisty, and they will freely challenge the status quo and those in authority.

True peace only exists in a stable world, in which as many societies as possible have reached a status resembling that blessed condition. In a stable society the people have institutions that will support prosperity and progress and that will be strong enough to manage the environment (everything they've been given to use and deal with), and especially the elements in the environment that threaten to degrade their society.

Even in a very stable society such as ours, the environment can throw a nasty blow that can send us reeling. In August 2005, Hurricane Katrina blasted through the central Gulf states, leveled significant parts of cities such as Biloxi, Mississippi, and annihilated New Orleans. Could the effects of this storm destabilize the United States? Hardly. But a natural disaster of that kind can seriously damage our most stable institutions. It can seriously harm our economy; it can traumatize a portion of the population; and it can cause the collapse of many of the local institutions that normally support the smooth running of a society. All these effects are made seriously worse if federal institutions are late to respond or if their actions turn out to be dysfunctional. Imagine how such a catastrophe plays out in the unstable parts of the world, where institutions are nowhere as formidable.

There aren't many parts of the world where human societies find it easy to survive. And it's hard to find a part of the world that is not vulnerable to hits from other societies or from nature . . . or sometimes from both in terrible combinations. Societies and nations need all the help they can get—from the environment they're blessed or cursed with and from the institutions they create . . . but also more and more from outside.

COBRA AND BEES

As 9/11 and Katrina have demonstrated, even the United States is not immune to big hits from enemies or from nature. There are bad moments even here, when even Americans do not find it easy to survive.

What are the new threats to our nation? Should we worry about chaos half a world away?

We already know that the world changed radically when the Soviet empire fell apart. Before, we had communism, the Cold War, and a stable—but high-risk—world order. Now we have globalization, the perfect storm, instabilities, and disorder.

We already know that the old ways of thinking about the world no longer apply. Communism and the near risk of nuclear Armageddon have lost their sting. The old tools we built at such enormous cost to combat the old threats are ineffective against the new ones. . . . And the new threats are confusing, nebulous, full of uncertainties.

As we face the new threats, we find ourselves in a variation of the old cliché: "Armies always fight the last war." We try to fight the last threats. As with much else in our national life, World War II provides the model . . . but with an added Cold War corollary.

In World War II we fought *The Totalitarian Threat.*

We adapted the model to the Cold War. Hegemonic, world-dominating communism became *the threat.* But since the force that the one monolithic threat could bring to bear against us, and that we could bring to bear against it, risked destroying all life on the planet, directly attacking the threat was not our best option. Instead, we chose to contain and deter the threat. And that worked.

There was a clear, irrefutable line from the threat to conflict to war to World War III—a world catastrophe. This Cold War corollary was added to the World War II model. According to the World War II/III model, the only threats that really count *must* be military (attack) or catastrophic (World War III); and they *must* be countered by the application of violent military force.

Let's face it: World War III no longer makes military planners desperately anxious (though it could conceivably break out if some regime possessing nuclear weapons goes totally insane); and other significant military threats to the United States are likely to be rare. No nation is going to invade the United States. No sane nation will even choose to take on the United States militarily in a conventional war. War with China is conceivable, but unlikely. War with North Korea is more likely, and the North Koreans might possibly deliver and set off a handful of nuclear devices in this country . . . but at the cost of overwhelming retaliation. Iran might pose a similar threat in a decade or two, but would face similar overwhelming costs. Other military threats? Unlikely.

Violent attacks, however, are not going away. Any organization that can successfully transform airliners into kamikaze missiles, killing thousands of people and toppling two of the world's tallest buildings can find other ways to wreak violent havoc. Al Qaeda or other terrorists might acquire weapons of mass destruction and use them here or in Europe.

Such events are grimly possible. The threats are real, and must be countered. But they are not the threats that are going to do us the gravest harm in this new, radically changed, globalized world.

What does the president of the United States worry about?

> He keeps telling us we are a nation at war.
> He keeps telling us he is anxious about our nation's physical security.
> He keeps telling us that terror is a threat.
> He keeps telling us he is worried about our economic well-being.
> He keeps telling us Social Security is going to run out of money.
> He keeps telling us we need a better energy policy.
> He keeps telling us that we need to worry about the cost of health care and the possibility that we will no longer be able to afford it.
> He keeps telling us we must deal with the illegal migrations crossing our borders.

Every problem in that list was either generated from the unstable part of the world or can be exacerbated by it. And he can make every problem on the list better or worse by dealing or not dealing with instabilities in the underdeveloped parts of the world.

The *real* threats do not come from military forces or violent attacks; they do not come from a nation-state or hostile non-state entity; they do not derive from an ideology (not even from a radical, West-hating, violent brand of Islam). The *real* new threats come from instability. Instability and the chaos it generates can spark large and dangerous changes anywhere they land.

I often talk to business, military, or veterans groups, trying to explain these issues. My audiences always understand instability and how instabilities can wreck a society. They feel sorry for the people in unstable countries who suffer the collapse of their worlds. But they don't see the instability over there as a threat over here. How is instability going to bite us? Where are its teeth?

I get this question again and again: "I hear you, General Zinni. What you're saying really makes sense. People are enduring terrible suffering. But so what? Do we need to do anything about that? No. That's nuts. Their catastrophe is never going to affect me. Where's the violent threat to me from that? What military threat does it pose? Are Syria and Iran and Afghanistan and Somalia and Zimbabwe going to form a grand coalition to invade the United States? We have plenty of worries here that require money and attention. Why should we spend our tax dollars to fix problems that in no way are our problems?"

After my formal presentation there's usually a social hour, when I can chat with members of the audience. Invariably, the same people who vehemently protest that instabilities over there will never touch us over here will start complaining: "Boy, can you believe the price of gas! If it goes up any more, I'll have to get rid of my SUV." Or: "Wow, I never thought I'd see so many new immigrants moving here into our community! Are they legally here?" Or: "The bus and subway bombing in London was terrible! I'm afraid to get on the train." Or: "The job situation is terrible in our town. The outsourcing to places with cheap labor is killing us. I'm in management; so I'll probably make out okay until I retire. But I worry about my kids. They might have to leave the state. Or if they stay, they may have to work at McDonalds."

After they've just strongly stated that nothing's bad, that all is right with their world, they then say that they are seriously uncertain about the future and worried about instability-related changes. Yet, they are unable to see how these worries contradict their initial perception that we have nothing much to worry about.

They see a partial truth: we probably won't get hit by a really big blow. Yes, the Cold War is over. We can no longer draw a clear, irrefutable line from here to catastrophe—to World War III. Violence may hit us—as it hit London in 2005, and as it hit us in 2001. But the violence will not be a World War III knockout blow.

What they don't see is *not* the big blow, but the hundreds of little ones. We are going to see changes. Instability-driven changes from around the world are going to wash onto our shores. Globalization and the perfect storm guarantee that. These changes can lead to all sorts of possibilities. No one can tell right now what possibilities or when, how they will affect us or how bad they will be. Yet it's certain that some of the changes will be significant and affect us. Our near-future is not going to be as good as we would like to think. And it may turn out to be terrible . . . even catastrophic. A lot of changes are swarming.

We're now in the position of the man who slept with a cobra. The cobra is gone. Now the room is full of bees. Could those bees kill him? Possibly. Possibly not. But even if they don't, they could make his life painful and miserable. Does it make sense, now that the cobra is gone, not to worry about the bees?

A sixty-five-year-old man has been looking forward all his life to retirement. His dream has been to buy a really nice RV and use it as a land yacht to tour the States and Canada. He worked all his life at the local auto parts plant, expecting to achieve his dream, which had been guaranteed by a lifelong promise of union benefits and a great retirement plan. The plant failed . . . closed. The parts manufacturer transferred the manufacturing end of the business to Malaysia. That wiped out the man's retirement plan. The town where he lives is in decline; it's losing businesses; it's losing population. Good jobs are ever more scarce. Property values have taken a dive. He can't give away the house he bought in 1976 and expected to sell for a big profit. He's in good health; he can expect to live another twenty years. To survive he's now flipping burgers and working a night job pumping gas. His dream is dead. To him, his life, everything he lived for, is ruined.

For him, globalization and the perfect storm caused a catastrophe as devastating as a bomb that blew away his house.

How many of those stories are going to happen? How many situations like that count up to a *real* catastrophe?

African hackers get into the Social Security system and destroy it. Social Security checks cease for six months. An elderly lady depends on her monthly check. It's her only income. Without it she can't pay the rent and will lose her apartment. Is this threat significant enough to make us worry?

An avian flu pandemic kills forty million people all over the world because the health services in Asian countries did not have the institutional strength and know-how to prevent it. Was Stalin right that the death of one person is a tragedy, the death of forty million a statistic?

Shia religious fundamentalists take over the oil-producing areas of the Persian Gulf (where lie most of the world's oil reserves). They decide to stop the evil West by cutting off their oil. When you can find it, gas costs $25 a gallon. The world economy collapses.

Pakistan breaks apart like the former Yugoslavia. Some of its nuclear weapons go missing, and are probably in the hands of Al Qaeda. Others are launched against Indian targets. The Indians strike back.

The Central Asian nations—the -Stans—fall into low-level warfare with one another. Hundreds of thousands of refugees flee.

Zimbabwe implodes into an orgy of genocidal killing like Rwanda's.

The effects of the perfect storm are not limited to people and places outside our borders. They can also come home. Global instability disrupts trade and investment, and the world economy takes a dive. I'm laid off; my wife is put on half-time; I can't pay for gas for my pickup; we can't pay our kids' college tuition and they can't get loans or other aid; they have to quit school; I get avian flu; a Hispanic gang floods the streets of my community with methamphetamines; and some angry Muslim blows up the mall in my neighborhood . . . the perfect storm.

The threats we face today are no longer monolithic—as they were in the Cold War. They don't all come together in one devastating catastrophe or from a single, powerful source. They're distributed; they're varied; they'll hit us from directions we won't expect; they'll hit us in unexpected places. They may or may not take a violent form. More likely, they will appear in messy businesses like failures in health care, migrations, economic dislocations, or job losses. None of these in and of itself has the potential to destroy our society, or to significantly affect it. But cumulatively they can have big-time effects.

It's the death of a thousand stings.

I may have to live in a smaller, meaner house. I may not be able to drive a big, comfortable car. I may not be able to go out to dinner at nice restaurants. I may no longer be able to put good, wholesome food on my table. I may no longer be able to take lovely vacations in Italy or France or Wyoming. My kids can no longer look to a better life than I had. I may have to lower all my expectations, because the nation can no longer compete, because other competitors are drawing away jobs and investments. All these changes will seriously and significantly affect our lives and our sense of security, economic well-being, and health.

Sure, there will be jobs for our children. Supermarkets, Wal-Mart, and Starbucks will be around. We can put brakes on immigrants taking our jobs by putting brakes on immigrants coming here. But that's not the life our children wanted or expected, or that they were promised.

Sure, our society will survive and continue. But our society will not continue as it now exists.

And yet well-meaning people keep telling me: "Well, there's no real military threat. There are no big time Armageddon-type catastrophes around the corner. Terrorism is scary, but I live in the heartland. They aren't going to hit me where I live."

It's like having five diseases, none of which will kill us, but all together can hurt us badly. They may even permanently—or irretrievably—damage us. But somehow we don't feel like doing anything about our condition: "Well, it's not cancer."

In many ways we're like Belle Époque Europe during the lead-up to World War I. "Don't worry. The nations are mobilizing, but that's no big deal. If the conflict gets serious, somebody will take care of it. Life is good. The empire is at peace and prosperous. We have no problems."

Yet, we may be incrementally moving toward catastrophe. But this time it will not be announced by the thunder of guns. It will be announced by the stings of bees.

We blind ourselves to the bad things coming. We go about our lives. Even when dangerous changes make their presence known, we ignore them as they get just a little bit worse and a little bit worse . . . like the frog in the pot of water who doesn't feel the water heating up.

Are we going to act to prevent catastrophe or not?

We have three choices, based on the following three projections:

One. The threats caused by instability will be temporary. The effects on the nation, if any, will be minor. We'll get through them without deep scars. And we will all continue to exist in the lifestyle we have now—with all the comforts, confidence, security, and economic well-being we feel we have a right to expect.

Two. The threats caused by instability will change us. We'll get through the next few years okay, but with scars and with significant negative changes to our society and in our comforts, confidence, security, and economic well-being.

Three. The threats caused by instability will pose a significant or perhaps even catastrophic challenge to our society. It will radically change our way of life for the worse.

One of these will happen; I can't tell you which.

If it's "One," then we can safely ignore instability. Our lives will continue down the happy path we've been traveling.

If it's—best case—"Two" or—worst case—"Three," instability will change our lives. The gravity of the changes will depend on the unpredictable nature of instability. We certainly don't want "Three" to happen. . . .

We have a choice. We can do all we can to create stability and order in the world. Or we can do nothing, hunker down, and gamble that the instability and chaos out there will not migrate over here—knowing that steel and electronic barricades will never seal our borders.

My experiences at CENTCOM led me to several conclusions that had been forming in my mind over my years of involvement in the most wobbly regions of the world. These same conclusions apply to the entire unstable world:

- The problems out there *will* come to affect all of us in the stable part of the world, and this is happening with ever-increasing frequency.
- It doesn't take much for unstable societies to fall over the edge.
- It doesn't take much to keep most of these societies from falling over the edge.
- The first world—the stable part of the world—has failed to understand the changes in the world over the last two decades; that makes this problem a growing danger to global stability and peace.

- It's hard to motivate the first world either to care about or to help resolve the instabilities in this region until conditions there degenerate into a catastrophe.
- We must understand this part of the world far better than we do now. We must understand especially why it's becoming a threat to global stability, and why it's in our interest to help bring stability there. And finally, we must understand what we need to do to help change things there and how we need to do it.

The entire world faces a choice: to put in the time, effort, and wisdom necessary to shape an order everyone can live with (as happened in Germany and Japan after World War II), or, to let nature take its course (as happened after World War I, when a near universal failure to take action allowed the Nazi "order" to emerge out of an unstable Germany).

The action needed is not some twenty-first-century rebirth of the White Man's Burden. Our job in the developed world is not to command and direct but to help, support, and empower. And there's a big place in this for every variety of actor: governments, regional organizations, international organizations, NGOs, ad hoc international coalitions, single individuals, groups and organizations within nations . . . anyone who wants to help, who can work with the others, and who can do the job effectively.

We must think of these actions not as "foreign aid" that tosses billions of dollars down some sinkhole of corruption but as investments in our own security and stability. By helping others—a good in itself—we are also greatly lessening the threats to our own well-being.

The invasion and occupation of Iraq has so far cost our nation something like $300 billion of our not-inexhaustible treasure, and over 2,000 American and *many* more Iraqi lives. Could we have put half that amount to better use in the years before September 2001, building stability and order in the region?

AMERICA MUST BE GOOD

We are the most powerful nation on the planet, with a set of values and laws we believe are unsurpassed. We are the City on the Hill. We offer societies in danger of failing a two-hundred-year tested model for security, peace, prosperity, governance, and hope. We can apply every dimension of our power to the task of building order, security, and peace virtually anywhere we choose (though not everywhere at once).

We can bring to that task diplomacy and mediation. We can bring capacity building, where we help create the rule of law and help develop essential institutions. We can bring in political processes. We can bring the capacity to distribute information to societies where information has been controlled, or where the infrastructure for delivering information is absent. We can bring in security capabilities. We can help provide order in its absence, and then construct a system that restores the society's ability to provide order. We can bring in economic assistance. We can bring in humanitarian assistance. We can help people work through social change. No nation has our power for good.

Yet, many of the world's peoples view the United States in a far-from-positive light. We would love to have our freedoms and our culture valued out there. And they're not. In much of the world they're seen as threatening. They breed hostility.

Why?

It's easy to write off hatred and call it envy. But hold on. A couple of years ago, in the aftermath of 9/11, the only people who hated us were the ones who planned and organized the attack, their friends, and anyone else who might not like us because our friends were their enemies. Even if we look farther back—a decade ago, say—the people who liked us far outnumbered the people who didn't.

What happened? If we can shape the environment out there, how come we can't inspire people to join us? How come we created hatred and distrust in many situations despite our good intentions?

I think we must face the reality that even though we are more than any other society in history capable of influencing the environment, that doesn't make us capable of controlling or creating it.

I think we must additionally face the reality that just as we don't know our own power or how to use it, we are not aware of the ways we actually touch, affect, or influence the environment.

Our leaders in Washington intend to build policies and take actions out in the world that will bring good results. Their motives are noble, generous, and charitable. Our leaders' error is their simplistic view of what is actually out there, their lack of understanding of the complexities, the fine points, the subtleties of conditions on the ground (an understanding that you get from long experience working in the foxhole).

Like all Americans, our leaders like clarity and simplicity in everything.

Americans are a sound-bite society. We want the weather in fifteen seconds. We want to get the news by skimming the top. We want issues to be simple. We want entertainment and not disturbing views of chaotic parts of the world. But that's not the way the world is.

So our leaders don't understand that setting this particular cause in motion may not produce the effect they intend, and may unleash even more unintended second- and third-order effects, or a cascading chain of events that could climax in catastrophe.

Achieving good results means more than acting from good and decent motives. It means knowing *how* to achieve the good results, from beginning to end. It means knowing what you have to do to get to the good results.

Americans have to realize that we can no longer thrive in isolation from an unstable world.

We have to realize that it is in America's interest not to have growing areas of this world sink into a sea of destabilizing conditions. The problems that result will be our problems. We are at a point in history when accomplishing good, noble, and altruistic goals also happens to accomplish the pragmatic goals that will promote our self-interest in survival, security, well-being, and future growth. In effect, it is a perfect storm that responds to the one that formed to threaten us. It is the convergence of the morally right and good with practical actions. We don't have to choose one or the other in a zero-sum game. It is in our best interest to have a stable, secure, prosperous world, because that is the world in which we best thrive.

To begin to create that kind of world will take significant changes in our thinking, organization, planning, and actions as we chart our national course through the uncertain conditions of a radically changed world.

Once upon a time, a long, long time ago, our nation could achieve peace, security, and prosperity by keeping ourselves isolated from the rest of the world. Isolation won't get us there anymore. It's a casualty of the passage of time. Isolation is no more viable in today's world than Jefferson's nation of yeoman farmers. It has become increasingly obvious that for us to prosper, for us to be secure, we must work to achieve a stable world. We can't leave unstable parts of the world unattended.

The "Battle for Peace" is not a battle in the classical sense—a battle that follows the sudden crisis blow that triggers a military conflict.

The battle is the constant struggle to develop and build the measures, programs, systems, and institutions that will *prevent* crisis. The battle is the constant struggle to shape and manage the harmful elements in the environment that generate instabilities.

The "Battle for Peace" is the battle to achieve a stable world.

INDEX

General Tony Zinni (Ret.) served as the Commander-in-Chief of U.S. Central Command (CENTCOM) from 1997 to 2000, responsible for all U.S. forces in a 25-country region, including the Middle East. He also served as Secretary of State Colin Powell's special envoy to Israel and the Palestinian Authority in 2002. General Zinni (with Tom Clancy) is coauthor of the New York Times *best-seller* Battle Ready. *He lives in Williamsburg, Virginia. Official U.S. Military photo.*